buy...

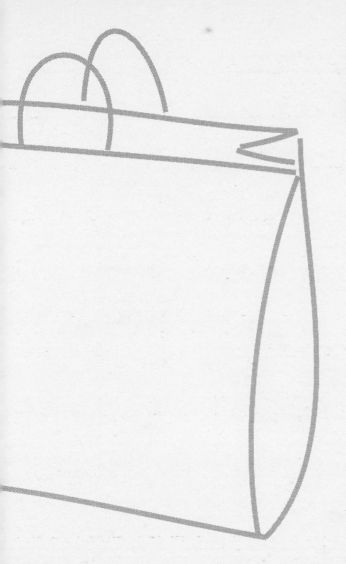

LEO HICKMAN

how to buy...

Atlantic Books
London

for Jane

acknowledgements

This book would never have reached your hands if the following people hadn't, each in their own way, contributed with their time, advice and expertise: Mathew Clayton, Ian Katz and Roger Browning at the *Guardian*; Alice Hunt, Toby Mundy and Neil Foxlee at Atlantic Books; all the experts – Alan Bamberger, Hannah Berry and everyone at *Ethical Consumer*, Sandy Boler, Ian Calcutt, Zac Goldsmith, Jamie Goode, Richard Hallett, everyone at *Drapers Record*, Matthew Line, Caroline Murphy, Catherine O'Dolan, David Orkin, Perdita Patterson, Scott Rowley, Paul Sanders, Rosemary Ward and Neil Whitford.

But, above all, Jane Crinnion – the world's best shopper.

Leo Hickman
London, March 2002

First published in 2002 by Atlantic Books, on behalf of Guardian Newspapers Ltd. Atlantic Books is an imprint of Grove Atlantic Ltd.

Copyright © Guardian Newspapers Ltd 2002

10 9 8 7 6 5 4 3 2 1

A CIP catalogue record for this book is available from the British Library

ISBN 1 84354 024 X

Printed in Great Britain by Mackays of Chatham Ltd

Designed by Bryony Newhouse

Atlantic Books
An imprint of Grove Atlantic Ltd
Ormond House
26–27 Boswell Street
London WC1N 3JZ

All information and contact details were correct, to the best of the author's and publisher's knowledge, at the time the book went to press.

contents

air travel   1

art   11

baby things   17

beds   26

bicycles   34

cameras   43

cars   51

computers   62

designer clothes   72

diamond rings   81

fridges, freezers and washing machines   89

furniture, fixtures and fittings   98

gym memberships   109

household electronics   116

kitchens and bathrooms   126

mobile phones   136

musical instruments   146

organic food   153

pets   160

plants   167

property   175

weddings   184

wine   193

air travel

the basics

The next time you board a plane, take a moment to look around at all the other passengers. There's a good chance that between all of you flying that day, you will have paid dozens of different prices for the luxury of being aboard that same speeding hunk of metal. It will be the same story when you check into your hotel or queue for your hire car. Due to the travel industry's competitiveness and complex structure, it can sometimes appear to be as familiar with the concept of fixed pricing as a hawker in a Moroccan souk.

Shopping around for the best price is never more rewarding than when booking air travel. This has been particularly true since 1997, when the EU reduced competitiveness restrictions and finally opened the door to the so-called budget airlines. For those determined to find the cheapest possible method of getting from A to B, times have never been better. And with the traveller's best friend – the internet – at hand, there really is no excuse not to be travelling on the lowest possible fares.

Homework is, as ever, your key to finding the best deal. There is clearly a big difference in booking a day-return business class flight for a meeting in Europe compared to a two-week family holiday in the sun, but as soon as you have some rough dates for travelling and a budget, you should set about reading up on your destination and all the different ways in which you can get there.

Beyond the wealth of newspaper travel sections and guide-books (all with their accompanying websites), such as those produced by Lonely Planet, Rough Guides, Fodor's, the AA and Michelin, it is often a good idea to take a look at the destination's tourist board website. Many of the better ones provide updated news about hotel and travel deals. *Travel Weekly*'s website – the UK travel industry's leading trade publication – has a comprehensive list of the world's tourist board sites (**www.travelweekly.co.uk**, click on 'Links'), as well as an exhaustive list of airline contact details. In addition, the *Guardian*'s Travel website has a very handy section (**www.guardian.co.uk/travel/cheapflights**), through which you can find out which airlines fly to which destination – particularly useful when flying to Europe or America, where competition is fierce.

Organizing visas, jabs, insurance and passports also usually requires plenty of time and attention. Many travel agents or officially sanctioned visa agents, such as the Visas Australia Company (tel: 01270 626626) will offer their assistance – for a fee – but again, if time is on your side, a combination of visiting the ever-useful Foreign Office website (**www.fco.gov.uk/travel**) and some browsing on travel insurance sites (**www.screentrade.co.uk** and **www.columbusdirect.co.uk** are good starting points) should enable you to keep costs down.

The bargain-obsessed frequent globetrotter could possibly try to get hold of or borrow the industry bible – the DG&G guides (**www.dggtravelinfo.co.uk** for details). These handy directories are used by most travel agents and list in detail who flies where, what hotels are available, and, in general, enable you to see a destination through the eyes of a travel agent. As with all industry guides and directories, they are very expensive (over £50 in most cases), but if you travel frequently or have a group of friends, colleagues or family who could share the cost, they could prove to be a valuable source of reliable information.

before you buy

On any one day, the world's airlines can make up to twenty thousand price changes to airfares. As a result, it's best to research prices for as long a period as possible, rather than just setting aside a couple of hours. The numerous 'special offers' and deals that the airlines make available, coupled with their careful 'yield management' (overbooking flights by a few per cent after predicting how many cancellations there are likely to be), mean that you must cast your net as wide as possible by ringing round travel agents, studying the Sunday newspaper travel ads and checking websites and Teletext.

Get as many quotes as possible, but be prepared to make a quick commitment to a good deal if you feel it is likely to be withdrawn shortly, even if it means paying a minimum deposit to secure the offer (usually about £50). Be flexible too, if possible. Can you stay over a weekend? Can you fly into any airport within a 150-mile radius of where you want to go? (There could be a significant difference in price, for example, between flying into San Diego or Los Angeles, even though they are only about an hour and a half's drive apart.) Can you fly at inconvenient times? Are you willing to have one or more transfers in addition to flying with any of the available airlines? Try ringing the travel agents and airlines as late or as early in the day as possible, when they may be less busy and thus have time to look more widely for deals. Once you've buttered them up with your civil and knowledgeable tone, ask them if they know of any upcoming deals – ones that haven't been advertised yet.

When considering the different offers available, also try to think laterally. One way of getting the best prices is to consider 'nested' or split tickets. Due to the peculiar way that a return can often be cheaper than a single, or a short break more expensive than a longer stay, these are always worth investigating.

This can cause a headache just trying to think about it, so remember: nested tickets only work when a regular midweek fare is more than twice the price of an excursion fare to the same destination that includes a Saturday stopover. If, for example, you've been quoted £150 for a Heathrow to Edinburgh return going out on a Monday and coming back on the Friday of the same week, but can find a return that requires you to stay for a weekend and is priced £75 or less, you've done it. Buy a £75 excursion return leaving on that Monday, but coming back late in the next week. Then buy another £75 excursion return, but with the outbound leg starting in Edinburgh.

This leg must be dated for the Friday you want to return to Heathrow on. The return leg should be dated early in the next week.

If you use the right coupons in the right order, you will actually get two return flights for the price of one. So if you nest the tickets carefully with future dates in mind, you can organize yourself an additional trip for no extra cost. Got all that?

Split tickets are much easier to organize. This is when you buy cheaper tickets that go via C, rather than straight from A to B, often with two different airlines. Most travel agents will be able to help you organize both nested and split tickets, but do always ask about them, as they may not publicize these deals. And don't forget to check with the charter airlines when looking for the best prices, as you'll be surprised how many destinations they fly to that aren't just typically holiday-oriented.

With budget airlines, you must book as early as possible for the best deals. Don't automatically assume that they are always the cheapest option, though, because their prices can sometimes become more expensive than the regular airlines as the departure date draws close.

Don't always be dazzled by flights priced at, for example, £1. The budget airlines rarely advertise all the taxes involved – usually about an extra £20 – until you are on the verge of making your purchase. Remember, too, to book online for extra discounts (usually only a few pounds).

Here are some tips to remember when booking a ticket to help you avoid delays and hopefully gain some legroom:

* Most of the major tour operators who have their own fleet, such as Thomson and JMC, now let you pre-book seats for a small fee (about £10) when buying a package holiday through them. They also often offer pricier supplements that give you better in-flight meals and extra legroom.

* Ask which type of plane you will be flying on when you book. Then look on the airline's website at the seat plans for their planes (many now provide this facility). If the airline will assign you a seat (nowadays a privilege that is only really open to Frequent Flyer or Air Miles scheme members – check with your credit card firm

or the airline for details), tell them what seat number you would ideally like – for example, an exit seat if you're after extra legroom.

* To avoid delays, try to book flights that are the first or last to leave an airport on that day. Also try to avoid 'code-sharing' tickets. This is when, even though it looks by the code on your ticket (e.g. BA123) that one airline is taking you all the way to your destination, two airlines actually perform the task. This comes about because many airlines now form alliances (the OneWorld Alliance, **www.oneworldalliance.com**, for example) and share the burden of getting you from A to B. Swapping baggage as well as yourself between different airlines at a stopover only increases the chances of things being delayed or going amiss, so look for the most direct flights if you want to minimize delays.

* Ask about the plane's 'seat pitch' in the class you're travelling. This is the distance between your seat and the one in front of it, namely, your legroom. Ergonomists believe that 31 inches should be the minimum for a 6-foot-tall person travelling on a long-haul flight.

getting an upgrade

Everyone's dream, but sadly never that likely. Most people have a theory on how to pull it off – looking the part, turning up really late to check in, putting a ring on your wedding finger and pretending you've just got married – but unless the sales manager on duty that day believes you warrant the magic SFU (Suitable For Upgrade) tag, usually saved for frequent fliers, then your best hope is being 'bumped'.

When the yield management calculations go wrong, as they do on busy routes, the airline must first ask all the passengers if anyone would like to volunteer to be bumped onto the next available flight. If you have time and flexibility on your side, this can be quite a lucrative option, as you are likely to get travel vouchers, cash, or possibly an upgrade, if the delay is more than several hours.

If it is less than that, all you will be offered is a phonecard, a food voucher, a temporary pass to the executive lounge, or if it's overnight, a room in some faceless airport hotel, so bargain hard to make sure you get something worthwhile. Ideally, you want travel vouchers, as they will always be worth more in face value than any cash offered to you. You do, however, have the right to demand cash.

buying from travel agents

Whether it's the high-street travel agent, or one that is on the other end of a phone, make sure they are registered with the Association of British Travel Agents (ABTA, **www.abta.com**), the industry's watchdog and safeguard against the rogue operators. Beware any advertising that says the agent is acting on behalf of an ABTA member. Check on the ABTA website that the membership codes advertised match up, if this is the case.

Some of us manage to find a trusted agent that we return to time and again, but it's always worth remembering that it's questionable whether an agent is working to your advantage or the airlines', especially when you consider that an airline will pay the agent about 10 per cent commission for securing you as a passenger.

It's worth asking whether you could save this money by shopping around with the airlines yourself. When you're speaking to an agent, watch out for vague promises of flying with a major airline or staying with a major hotel chain. You want to have precise details right from the start. Don't be tempted by other classic 'bait and switch' techniques that aim to lure you in, for example the ever-so-enticing two-for-one offer or discount that draws you in, but has miraculously sold out, or has reams of accompanying small print and strings attached.

It could also be worth paying for your travel arrangements with a credit card to help protect you against insolvencies and rogues. Many credit cards also now offer free travel insurance, but check the details to make sure the cover is adequate.

If you are tempted by offers in the Sunday papers from consolidators who bulk-buy seats on planes – better known as bucket shops – consider them, but don't stop shopping around, and make sure that what's on offer is covered by the ABTA code. Be particularly careful if you are going for last-minute deals.

Other ways of saving money by cutting out the middleman:

* Brochure prices for holidays can nearly always be bettered by booking the flight and accommodation yourself, particularly for mid-range and luxury-priced holidays.

* If you work for a large firm or are a member of a union, ask the department that coordinates travel, or the union representative, if they can help you get a good deal through their preferred agent. You may benefit from the privileges earned from them being a bulk buyer.

* Most city breaks in Europe can now be easily arranged by yourself, because of the wide choice of destinations offered by the budget airlines. Booking hotels is now easier than ever, because most have websites and accept email or phone bookings. Just check the hotels against guidebook recommendations to make sure you get what you paid for. However, the agents often get you the best last-minute city-break deals.

* Have you thought about being a courier? It's not as popular as it used to be, but carrying an item in your luggage for a business to another country can save you at least £100 on most flights. However, you need to be ultra flexible as well as a lone traveller, which means that it only tends to be favoured by backpackers.

buying from the web

Now that the computer reservation systems that travel agents used to keep to themselves (such as Sabre, Galileo, Apollo, Worldspan and Amadeus) are accessible on the net via online agents, it seems odd that anyone would not prefer to key in the date and destination themselves rather than pay someone else to do it for them.

If you go to any of the big comparison sites, such as Expedia or Travelocity, in addition to visiting all the sites of the airlines that go to your destination, you can soon see a breakdown of who is flying where, for what prices and when. As long as you make sure that the flight is covered by ATOL (Air Travel Organizers' Licensing, **www.atol.org.uk**) and that you stick to the well-known, UK-based sites (look for a UK postal address on the site that isn't just a PO Box number), you should be fine. Again, it may add an extra level of

expert view

Tips for buying long-haul flights by David Orkin, who is now a travel writer, but who previously spent sixteen years working for Trailfinders and Quest Worldwide Travel (of which he was a director).

- Traditional high-street travel agents have their uses, but go to a specialist for discounted long-haul flights: they will be aware of more options, be more knowledgeable on the subject, and offer more competitive prices.

- The internet is good for short-haul destinations and can be good for straightforward point-to-point long-haul fares. However, I have yet to see a website that can begin to cope with multi-stop itineraries, or one which can say (as a good agent should), 'By the way, there's a better fare if you go a couple of days earlier/later', or offer other suggestions.

- It should be obvious, but if you use www.priceline.co.uk, there's no going back once your offer is accepted by the airline. There are no grounds for complaint if you could have found cheaper flights elsewhere.

- Many agents – even those with offices outside the M25 – automatically assume that you want to fly from London. Before you book, ask your agent to compare costs from London and from your nearest regional airport.

- Paying a deposit doesn't guarantee a fare. Although the specialist agents always endeavour to notify clients when advised of imminent fare increases, be prepared to be contacted at any time between paying your deposit and the 'Balance Due By' date, and asked to pay up to secure your fare.

- Be aware that it can be free, or cost very little extra, to travel on to points other than your main destination, but these options aren't always offered and have to be asked for. For example, if you're travelling to Kuala Lumpur, you may well be given a fare on Malaysia Airlines by an agent. Its fare to Singapore is usually identical (except for a few pounds extra in taxes), but offers a stop in KL in each direction. In other words, you can get a return flight to KL with a (virtually) free side-trip to Singapore.
  Similarly, though very competitive, Qantas aren't always the cheapest airline to Australia. However, if you're intending to take domestic flights in Australia it might be possible to include these in your international fare for relatively little extra.

- It may well be worth signing up if the airline you're flying with offers a free 'loyalty' scheme. Two completed long-haul round-trip flights – sometimes just one – can earn you enough points/air miles for a free ticket or other privileges. Programmes differ from airline to airline, but I have found Continental's OnePass scheme to be one of the most generous.

safety if you pay by credit card and always make sure that the site's server is secure by looking for the locked padlock symbol on your browser. (Look for an 'https' address rather than the normal 'http' once you enter the payment area of the site – it means the server is secure.)

Once you have paid for a ticket, you should receive an email within a few minutes confirming the details. This email is legally required to confirm your ATOL protection.

It may also be worth visiting **www.priceline.co.uk**, which allows you to offer your own price for flights. Airlines will look at your offer, and if you have pitched a reasonable price and they have the capacity, will sell you a ticket. Don't bid ridiculously low, though, as it will be rejected straight away. Try going in at about 20 to 30 per cent lower than the regular advertised fare. Remember, however, that most flights offered have severe restrictions (inconvenient departure times, for example), so check the small print carefully.

Increase your chances of getting to the best offers first by signing up to the email mailing lists of the airlines. Try visiting **www.ukfrenzy.co.uk** on a regular basis, too. This site monitors the internet for any coupon-code-type deals and has a special travel section listing all the airlines' current special offers.

Finally, it sometimes pays off to check the various travel news-groups to see if anyone has spotted a good deal. Go to **www.deja.com** and begin by searching for 'rec.travel' or 'rec.travel.air'. If you have a particular query, don't be afraid to ask all the other users for advice.

PRIMARY RESOURCES

ONLINE FARE SEARCHERS AND TRAVEL AGENTS

www.airnet.co.uk
www.bargainholidays.com
www.bridgetheworld.co.uk
www.cheapflights.com
www.deckchair.com
www.ebookers.com
www.expedia.co.uk
www.flightline.co.uk
www.flynow.com
www.lastminute.com
www.majortravel.co.uk
www.opodo.co.uk
www.otc-uk.com
www.skydeals.co.uk
www.statravel.co.uk
www.teletextholidays.co.uk
www.telmeglobaltraveller.com
www.thefirstresort.com
www.thomascook.co.uk
www.trailfinders.co.uk
www.travelocity.co.uk
www.travelselect.com

COURIERS

Air Courier Association
  tel: 001 800 282 1202
  www.aircourier.org

International Association of Air Travel Couriers
  tel: 0800 0746 481
  www.aircourier.co.uk

AIRLINES (OUT OF UK)

Aer Lingus
www.aerlingus.ie

Aeroflot
www.aeroflot.co.uk

Air 2000
www.air2000.com

Air Canada
www.aircanada.ca

Air China
www.air-china.co.uk

Air France
www.airfrance.com

Alitalia
www.alitalia.co.uk

Air India
www.airindia.com

Air Jamaica
www.airjamaica.com

Air New Zealand
www.airnewzealand.co.uk

Airtours
www.airtours.co.uk

All Nippon Airlines (ANA)
www.ana-europe.com

American Airlines
www.aa.com

Austrian Airlines
www.aua.com

Bmibaby
www.bmibaby.co.uk

British Airways
www.britishairways.com

Britannia
www.britanniaairways.com

British Midland
www.britishmidland.co.uk

Buzz
www.buzzaway.com

Cathay Pacific
www.cathaypacific.com

Continental Airlines
www.continental.com

CrossAir
www.crossair.com/en

Cyprus Airways
www.cyprusair.com.cy

Czech Airlines
www.czechairlines.co.uk

Delta Airlines
www.delta.com

easyJet
www.easyjet.com

El Al
www.elal.com

Emirates
www.emirates.com

Finnair
www.finnair.fi

Go
www.go-fly.com

Gulf Air
www.gulfairco.com

Iberia
www.iberia.com

IcelandAir
www.icelandair.co.uk

Japan Airlines
www.jal.co.jp

Kenya Airways
www.kenya-airways.com

Korean Airlines
www.koreanair.com

KLM
www.klmuk.com

Lufthansa
www.lufthansa.co.uk

Malaysia Airlines
www.malaysiaairlines.com.my

Manx Airlines
www.manx-airlines.com

Monarch
www.monarch-airlines.com

Northwest Airlines
www.nwa.com

Pakistan International
www.piac.com.pk

Qantas
www.qantas.com.au

Qatar Airways
www.qatarairways.com

Royal Air Maroc
www.royalairmaroc.com/ver_en

Ryanair
www.ryanair.ie

Scandinavian Airlines
www.scandinavian.net

Singapore Airlines
www.singaporeair.com

South African Airways
www.flysaa.com

Turkish Airlines
www.turkishairlines.com

United Airlines
www.ual.com

Virgin Atlantic
www.virgin-atlantic.com

VLM
www.vlm-airlines.com

art

the basics

The first and most widely touted rule of buying art is to put aside immediately any notion that it will ever be a good investment. Art is a notoriously fickle market best left to London's Cork Street professionals. The chances of one of your progeny turning up on the *Antiques Roadshow* in fifty years' time with your purchase and expressing surprise when told, 'for insurance purposes', to move it to a bank vault is next to zero. The most important factor when buying a work of art should be that you fall in love with it first.

Ask yourself: can you imagine it above the bed, or on the wall next to the TV? Will it suit your home's colour scheme? Are you happy to have this art as a fixture in your life in the months and years ahead? And are you absolutely sure you can afford it? After all, you are about to make a sizeable dent in your precious disposable income, not make a savings deposit.

With this in mind, you can now set about dipping your toes in the art market. It is admittedly an intimidating arena – all those 'By Appointment Only' galleries and exhibition openings crammed full of people sipping warm Pinot Grigio – but for first-time buyers it is easier, and often best, just to bypass galleries altogether.

There are a variety of alternative routes to buying art, but you should familiarize yourself with what's available before you take the plunge. Get out and do your homework: fine-tune your taste; visit a fine art graduate degree show; attend a local art fair; log on to some respected online galleries; flick through some of the contemporary art magazines. You will soon establish what you like and what's realistically available for your budget.

'Define, select, research and buy,' says Alan Bamberger, the US author of *Buy Art Smart* and the widely syndicated Art Talk column. Define what you like. Select the best practitioners. Research the current market. And, yes, then finally buy it.

Although art should never be seen as an investment, there are, however, a few tricks of the trade for reducing the chance of buying a piece that is superficially attractive, but is actually a worthless turkey. Bamberger recommends selecting typical rather than atypical works. Establish which subjects, mediums, sizes and styles your preferred artist is best known for. Leave their, let's say, experimental dalliances to others.

Also avoid artists that borrow heavily from (never say copy) the styles of celebrated artists of the past. We've already had one Pollock; you don't need a load of sub-standard Pollocks, do you?

Quality, though, should always hold its price. Look for high standards of draughtsmanship and skilled paintwork. Will Ramsay, the organizer of the Affordable Art Fair, says that the trend in the 1990s for shocking conceptual work is now over. Today's tastes are generally more conservative. Well-executed figurative and landscape paintings are always popular at Ramsay's fairs, but he recommends that you should always hunt down the most 'interesting and intriguing'.

If an original work proves to be beyond your budget (any oil painting, for example, is likely to cost, at the very least, several hundred pounds), it's worth considering buying a print, as they usually provide a much cheaper entry-point. You must, however, make sure you know the difference between an original print and a straight reproduction. An original print will have been produced by the artist, signed and limited to a relatively small number of copies. Ramsay warns that you should be sceptical of any print series that extends beyond 150 in number, as the plates from which prints are produced will often show signs of deterioration beyond this point.

Once you have found something you love, don't forget that payment arrangements can often be flexible in the art market. Don't

seeing red

Beware the red spot. Denoting that a work has been sold by placing a small red sticker by its side is common practice in the art world. It is more often than not an entirely innocent way of indicating that a work is sold, but it can also be used as a clever sales tool. Some dealers place red spots next to unsold works in order to give the impression that the artist's works are popular and selling well. This is especially useful with prints, where a handful of red dots next to the work will be a powerful thumbs-up to any doubting buyers. Try not to be influenced by a sea of red. The first rule still applies: make sure you love what you're about to buy.

hesitate to ask whether paying in instalments is an option. Many artists and dealers will also allow you to buy 'on consignment', that's to say, to try it at home for a week or two to see whether you really have made the right decision. Asking for a reduction is an option too, but don't abuse this right.

And always ask for a detailed receipt. Provenance is an important aspect of the art market. If you ever do decide to sell in the future, you will want to answer all the who? when? where? questions that you will be asked, and give the necessary proof. For this reason, it is worth collecting, in writing if possible, as much anecdotal information about the work as possible. Who's the portrait of? Where and when was this landscape painted? Where has the artist studied and exhibited?

expert view: how not to buy art

Alan Bamberger is an independent US appraiser and consultant specializing in fine art. He is the author of *Buy Art Smart* and offers advice at **www.artbusiness.com**.

- Don't buy art at night. The chances of buying art impulsively are greater at night than they are during the day. You'll tend to be less focused on rational, practical issues and more interested in entertaining yourself and having a good time.

- Don't buy art while you're on holiday. That painting of Parisian nightlife or a Greek sunset is sure to end up where you put that ebony carving from Nairobi market and the porcelain horse from Spain – in the attic.

- Don't buy art by name only. Never be star-struck by an artist's reputation.

- Don't buy art when the seller lowers the price drastically. Ask yourself why they're doing this. Why are they so desperate for a sale?

- Don't buy art under pressure. Ignore the dealer who stands over your shoulder. You need space and time to make your choice.

- Think twice before buying art for sale in restaurants, hotels and department stores. Try to confine your buying to professionals whose only business is buying and selling art.

- Don't buy art based on predictions. Be suspicious when dealers begin talking about what's supposed to happen with art or a given artist in the future.

- Beware the exhibition opening. Everything about the environment – the 'hip crowd', the wine, the nibbles, the music – is designed with one thing in mind: to sell you art.

- Don't be a silent customer. When you visit galleries, shows and fairs, don't be afraid to introduce yourself, ask questions and state what you're looking for.

on the web

Viewing contemporary art on the internet is popular because it eliminates that cringe factor many people feel when entering a gallery. But while it is the great leveller of the art world, it also has considerable drawbacks. Remember that whatever you see online is likely to have its apparent quality increased when seen at a thumbnail scale. Use the internet as a sourcing tool and avoid buying 'sight unseen'. There should never be a substitute for seeing the real artwork in a bricks-and-mortar environment. There are, however, a number of high-quality sites around that are certainly worth a browse, if only to see what's around and at what price:

www.artlondon.com
A large, high-end site, but its biggest draw is that it allows you to commission a portrait by artists such as Christian Furr, who is the youngest artist ever to have officially painted the Queen.

www.britart.com
Has a gimmicky but fun feature that decides what styles you may like, depending on what media you 'associate yourself with'. Are you a *Home & Gardens* / Radio 4 person, or a *Dazed & Confused* / E4 type?

www.countereditions.com
Certainly beyond the average budget, but worth a look if only because it's the online home to such BritArt luminaries as Tracy Emin, Chris Ofili, Sarah Lucas and Rachel Whiteread.

www.eyestorm.com
Again, this site is not for the budget shopper, but interesting because it has exclusive alliances with the Saatchi Gallery in London and the world-renowned Magnum photographic archive. Fantasize that some day you could afford just one of the Helmut Newtons, Damien Hirsts or Jeff Koons for sale.

www.insidespace.com
Another popular London gallery that now displays much of its stock online. Has recently opened an affordable gallery on the ground floor at Selfridges in London.

www.the-e-gallery.co.uk
Specialists in the work of recent graduates and arranging commissions.

www.whitecube.com
Online incarnation of celebrated east London gallery and home to many YBAs (Young British Artists), such as Gavin Turk, Antony Gormley and Sam Taylor-Wood.

art fairs

Art fairs provide the opportunity to see hundreds of different artists under one roof, and thus are perfect for judging, at a glance, what's on the market. Crucially, they often cater almost exclusively for the limited-budget buyer. Bear in mind, too, that they can be expensive for dealers to exhibit at, which can mean unannounced reductions towards the end of the fair, when dealers look to recoup their costs. Ask the dealer if that's 'their best offer', before rejecting something because it seems too pricey.

The Affordable Art Fair

tel: 0870 739 9555
www.affordableartfair.co.uk

Organized by Will Ramsay of Will's Art Warehouse in Fulham, London, the AAF is the self-proclaimed Oddbins of art fairs ('we sell the equivalent on canvas of a £5 to £10 bottle of wine'). There are no reproductions and everything costs under £2,500. Appears a handful of times a year at cities such as Bristol, Bath and London.

Art Futures

tel: 020 7831 7311
www.contempart.org.uk/
    artfutures.htm

The Contemporary Art Society's annual 'art market' offers works from recent fine art graduates. Prices range from £150 to £3,000, and profits help the society raise money to purchase works of art for museums throughout Britain. Last held at the Barbican Exhibition Centre in London, but contact the Society for information on future events.

Art on Paper Fair

tel: 020 8742 1611
www.artonpaper.co.uk

Dozens of dealers show works on paper from a wide range of periods, but including modern British drawings and watercolours. Held in the second week of February at the Royal College of Art in London, this fair is now in its fourth year. Prices start at £50.

Beatrice Royal

tel: 023 8061 0592
www.beatriceroyal.com

Not strictly an art fair, Beatrice Royal is more of an art supermarket. Located in Eastleigh, Hampshire, it is a not-for-profit, Lottery-funded mega-gallery set up in 1984 with the aim of making contemporary art more accessible and easier to buy.

20/21 British Art Fair

tel: 020 8742 1611
www.britishartfair.co.uk

Held in September at the Royal College of Art in Kensington, the fair shows British art from 1900 to the present day. Many big names such as Bacon, Freud and Hepworth feature, so it's no surprise that prices range from 'hundreds of pounds to many thousands'.

Fresh Art

tel: 0870 736 3108
www.freshartfair.co.uk

The London Art Fair's younger sibling. Also held at the Business Design Centre, but during mid-July, Fresh Art claims to be the only UK fair that exclusively displays independent artists, studio groups and graduates.

Glasgow Art Fair

tel: 0141 552 6027
www.glasgowartfair.com

This event is the largest contemporary art fair outside London and features up to forty selected galleries. Held during April in a marquee in George Square.

The London Art Fair

tel: 0870 739 9500
www.art-fair.co.uk

An annual fair held in mid-January at the Business Design Centre, Islington, London. It claims to be the UK's largest and hosts around one hundred galleries. Its Start section offers work by new graduate artists. Certainly not for the budget shopper, but a fair of very high standards.

degree shows

Not quite the bargain hunter's dream of urban myth, but still an exhilarating way to buy contemporary art. Degree shows usually take place in the summer months, and you can find the nearest to you by searching on **www.degreeshow.com**. Alternatively, ring your local art college. Try and find out beforehand what styles the college's students typically practise. There is a big difference in look between the work of students from, say, Goldsmiths and the Royal Academy of Arts. Are you looking for more traditional works or high-concept pieces?

The hottest tickets are always the relatively rare MA shows, due to the sensible theory that if an artist has got as far as completing an MA, there's a good chance they have staying power. It will, of course, mean higher prices, and it's not uncommon for artists to raise their prices for degree shows in the knowledge that, for once, the spotlight is on them. Remember that most artists will entertain a commission if all their work has sold out. They have student debts to pay off, after all.

The institutions listed here [▷] hold what are widely believed to be the highest-quality degree shows.

Birmingham Institute of Art & Design
www.biad.uce.ac.uk

Central Saint Martin's College of Art and Design
www.csm.linst.ac.uk

Chelsea College of Art & Design
www.chelsea.linst.ac.uk

Falmouth College of Arts
www.falmouth.ac.uk

Glasgow School of Art
www.gsa.ac.uk

Goldsmiths College
www.goldsmiths.ac.uk

Royal Academy of Arts
www.royalacademy.org.uk

Royal College of Art
www.rca.ac.uk

The Slade School of Fine Art
www.ucl.ac.uk/slade

Wimbledon School of Art
www.wimbledon.ac.uk

Winchester School of Art
www.wsa.soton.ac.uk

PRIMARY RESOURCES

For advice and news on the art market and recent sales, check the following publications:

AN, the Artist's Newsletter
tel: 0191 241 8000
www.anweb.co.uk

Antiques Trade Gazette
tel: 020 7420 6600
www.atg-online.com

Art Monthly
tel: 020 7240 0389
www.artmonthly.co.uk

The Art Newspaper
tel: 020 7735 3331
www.theartnewspaper.com

Art Review
tel: 020 7236 4880
www.art-review.co.uk

Frieze
tel: 01795 414977
www.frieze.com

Galleries
tel: 020 8740 7020
www.artefact.co.uk

Tate Magazine
tel: 020 7906 2002
www.tatemag.com

ONLINE DIRECTORIES OF UK ART GALLERIES

www.art-connection.com
www.artgalleries-london.com
www.newexhibitions.com

For further information about the contemporary art market, contact the following trade associations:

Association of Art and Antiques Dealers
tel: 020 7823 3511
www.lapada.co.uk

British Art Market Federation
tel: 020 7839 7163

Contemporary Art Society
tel: 020 7831 7311
www.contempart.org.uk

Fine Art Trade Guild
tel: 020 7381 6616
www.fineart.co.uk

baby things

the basics

Having children may leave you short of cash, but it certainly won't leave you short of advice. If it's not your parents, siblings, neighbours, friends and work colleagues offering their universal parenting truths, it's parenting magazines, TV shows and, er…newspaper articles and books. As all parents will testify, advice seems to just seep from the walls the moment you announce a little one is on the way. While most of this will, of course, be invaluable and especially appreciated by first-time parents, there is always a danger of being overwhelmed. Add to this the – let's admit it – competitive nature of parenting and the misinformation this can generate, and you can see why we still end up buying inappropriate things for our children.

Trendy fads don't help, either. Perhaps the best example is the three-wheel buggy craze that swept all before it a few years ago. One snapshot of Tom Cruise jogging through Central Park with one, and mothers from Winchester to Wichita fought to be the first to be seen pushing one down at the local park. Perceived wisdom (read day-nursery gossip) was that these contraptions were better than conventional pushchairs. However, after a few weeks of use, parents were soon cursing how heavy, immobile and – yes – expensive these pesky things were.

Thrifty spending is a key consideration at the best of times, but when you consider that a baby will cost you about £3,000 in its first year alone (some swear it's at least double that figure by the time you throw in childcare costs and the odd trip or three to BabyGap), you will want to start researching those 'best buys' as soon as the coal-and-gherkin sandwich cravings start. Even though a lot of 'essential' purchases can be put off until well after the birth, there are a handful of items – baby monitor, baby bath, carrycot, a job lot of nappies, clothing, bedding – that you really do need to have bought before bringing baby home. And guess what? That's likely to be another £1,000 you will need to find.

Once baby is up and tottering around your dry-clean-only, pastel furniture in search of more exhilarating entertainment than that offered by a wind-up mobile, the ante is upped by the prospect of having to buy toys, educational or otherwise, in addition to the basics such as food, clothing and 'baby gear'. And, friends and family take note, those cute fluffy bears that flooded in after the birth will certainly not be up to the job: baby is going to be on the hunt for things that are brightly coloured, interactive and offer a surmountable challenge.

If all this sounds daunting, well, welcome to parenting. The best general advice is to keep informed by sticking to trusted sources – favourite parenting magazines and websites, fellow parents with children of a similar age – and to research your big buys such as pushchairs and car seats carefully for price, but above all quality and usability.

food

Yes, admittedly it's essential, but after a few months of breast milk or formula you will soon be rueing the cost of those cute little jars of baby food. Full marks to the parents who have the time and fore-thought to pre-cook food and freeze it in ice-cube trays as the manuals so righteously recommend, but chances are you will end up buying them, even if it's just for convenience's sake when you're out and about.

There isn't really a trick to bargain-buying baby food other than, perhaps, bulk-buying a pallet of the stuff from a supermarket or cash-and-carry-type outlet. What is important, however, is that you examine the food's ingredients carefully beforehand. It is well publicized that baby food should not contain salt and large amounts of added sugar, but there are other additives that should be avoided. When you read a label, the order of the ingredients is important, as they should be listed according to percentage by volume. Watch out for large amounts of starch and water compared to the advertised principal ingredient. Look out for gluten and thickeners, such as gum and maltodextrin. All of this can be used to bulk out the main ingredient.

Organic baby food has understandably seen an explosion in sales over the last decade, even though there are now extremely strict controls on the use of baby food ingredients grown with pesticides. The most popular brand, Hipp, accounts for about 60 per cent of all organic baby food sales (about 10 per cent of the whole market), but dozens of other brands exist and are possibly cheaper. Even with organic food, however, you should still carefully examine the ordering of ingredients.

For exhaustive organic baby food reviews and advice, get hold of *The Organic Baby Book* by Tanyia Maxted-Frost (£7.95, Green Books, **www.theorganicbabybook.co.uk**).

toys

All those well-intended plans to allow your child to play only with educational toys will soon wither once they discover 'pester power'. The typical child will see up to fifty forms of advertising per day, be it on television or cereal packets, and half of all toys sold are associated through licensing with some kind of popular film or TV show like *Toy Story* or *Teletubbies*. That all adds up to a lot of pestering.

Every parent will have a different view on how to restrict this influence, but when buying toys, one consideration overrides everything – safety. Toys sold in the UK should all meet basic BSI (British Standards Institute) safety standards, but every Christmas, horror stories abound about imported toys that can choke or injure young children. You should, therefore, do your own safety checks when buying toys, particularly for babies and toddlers. Look out for sharp edges and small parts that will break off easily. Don't be tempted to buy a toy for a child younger than the toy's recommended age, even if you do think they are a budding Einstein.

Suitability is also important. Babies will always love gaudy colours and contrasting textures, but once they are crawling and itching to walk, mobile construction toys like a trolley with bricks are much loved. All sorting and construction toys, such as Lego's baby range, will be played with endlessly. And dress-up, role-playing and creative toys, such as Play-Doh, will be popular with toddlers and beyond too.

Be careful, though, if you are considering buying a toy chest to help regain some semblance of order back into your life. You will want to find one that has a hinge that prevents it slamming shut onto little fingers.

equipment

If you don't know how much kit a modern baby seems to need, visit an airport departure lounge. You will soon see families struggling with all manner of equipment such as pushchairs, carrycots, car seats – and that's in addition to all the bags of bedding, clothes, nappies, bottles, toys and other essentials. Some of the accessories that we buy for babies are probably of questionable use, but a handful are absolutely vital.

Pushchairs and car seats are going to require the biggest outlay of all. Pushchairs, in particular, need considerable research and thought before you take the plunge. Think really hard about your needs. Do you need to walk up stairs to your home? How big is your car's boot? Will you be using public transport frequently? The pushchair's weight, 'foldability' and mobility all need to be assessed, but it is best to read through as many product reviews as you can beforehand. Most parenting magazines and websites carry frequent reviews, as do the Consumer Association's *Which?* reports (**www.which.net**), but good things to look out for with pushchairs, for example, include front wheels that swivel, wheels that cannot puncture, pushchairs that let babies lie flat, and ones that can easily be carried in one hand when folded.

You may be tempted to get one of the new combination pushchairs that can be turned into a car seat and carrycot, but remember that it is unlikely to perform all its tasks as well as stand-alone models. And think twice before spending hundreds of pounds on all the matching accessories, such as rain covers, parasols, foot muffs and changing bags. Do you really need them all?

nappies and clothing

One of the biggest dilemmas you face with a newborn child is what type of nappy you use. Every day in the UK, we throw away nine million disposable nappies, which account for around 4 per cent of all household waste. When you consider that it is estimated that a disposable nappy can take up to five hundred years to decompose, it quickly becomes apparent what a scourge on the environment nappies have become.

Many parents are keen to counter this by using reusable nappies, but the effort and time required don't fit in too well with our convenience culture. The commitment is certainly financially rewarding, however. Just in the first year of a baby's life, you will save hundreds of pounds if you use reusable nappies, even if you use one of the nappy laundry services that are becoming popular among urban families.

Some parents choose to use a combination of both types of nappy to suit their needs. If you do want to try some disposable nappies, get hold of the many freebie trial packs from supermarkets and nappy companies to find out which brand suits your baby's skin and size. Getting a cheap or ill-fitting brand may prove to be a false economy, however, if you end up having to buy barrier cream to ease rashes. Seek further advice from the Real Nappy Association (www.realnappy.com).

The clothing you dress your child in is obviously a personal choice, but here the hand-me-down culture should be exploited to the full. Expensive trips to BabyGap and alike may be tempting, but you will save hundreds of pounds if you use clothing handed down to you or bought second-hand.

buying from the high street

Hiking up and down a high street with a baby is most people's idea of hell, but to make life a little easier on yourself, get hold of your local Baby Directory, or look at it online at **www.babydirectory.com**. Each directory lists all your local baby goods shops and will help you to quickly source the best places in your area. Websites such as **www.all4kidsuk.com** can also help you find nearby shops.

Most of us, of course, rely on the big supermarkets, which now fight among themselves to attract parent shoppers, especially mothers, with special offers, changing facilities and extra staff to help you. While supermarkets remain good places to bulk-buy some of the basics such as baby food and nappies, department stores and specialist shops should be your point of call for equipment and toys. Mothercare, Boots, and Mamas and Papas are all good solid starting

ethics watch

When *Ethical Consumer* investigated toy manufacturers, the main issue of concern was subcontracting in countries with poor human rights records. Readers concerned about exploitative labour practices were advised to avoid toys sourced from oppressive regimes such as China and Indonesia.

The magazine also recommended avoiding toys containing PVC. Some of the chemicals added to PVC, which may leak out if chewed, have been linked by groups such as Greenpeace to serious health and developmental problems in children. The magazine therefore advised shoppers to look for toys made by smaller companies, particularly those using traditional materials.

Taking into account the records of the producers on a range of social and environmental issues, the magazine's Best Buy advice was to choose Lego, as the company has a code of conduct on workers' rights and has made a commitment to phasing out its use of PVC.

When *Ethical Consumer* magazine examined baby

equipment, again, the main concern was manufacturers using labour in China, where there are regular violations of workers' rights. One of the manufacturers attracting the most attention from campaigners was Chicco. In 1993, a fire at a factory in China that made toys for Chicco killed eighty-seven people because the management had locked the gates to stop workers leaving.

Readers particularly concerned about environmental issues were also advised to seek out second-hand (recycled) equipment because of resource implications. Second-hand car seats, though, were not recommended, because any previous accident can limit effectiveness.

Taking into account the records of the producers on a range of social and environmental issues, the report's overall Best Buy advice was to choose baby equipment made by Britax, Klippan, Mamas and Papas, Silver Cross, Cindico or Maclaren.

For more information, visit www.ethicalconsumer.org or call 0161 226 2929.

points, but larger stores such as John Lewis arguably offer better customer care and may even offer a wider selection.

Out-of-town factory outlets offer an alternative to the high street, especially for clothing at bargain prices (you can locate them via www.shoppingvillages.com). And if you can manage it, a cross-Channel shopping trip will easily pay for itself in savings if you bulk-buy. Children's clothes, for example, are much cheaper in France.

from the web and catalogues

Is there a more useful invention for the housebound parent than internet shopping? Well, mail-order catalogues run it pretty close. Both offer extreme convenience and, in many cases, the best value.

Catalogues have long been a favourite read for parents. Popular ones such as *JoJo Maman Bébé*, *Blooming Marvellous* and Tesco's *Baby and Toddler* all now have an online presence for extra convenience. For a full list of UK mail-order catalogues for baby and children's goods, visit www.catalink.net, or www.cataloguecity.co.uk.

Some of the parenting advice websites also offer discounts at certain retailers: www.mumsnet.com, for example, offers 10 per cent off selected retailers when you sign up (for free). There are also many dedicated children's goods online retailers, a directory of which can be found at www.ukchildrensdirectory.com.

As ever, ask about and calculate the delivery costs and times. Try to stick to the well-known, trusted sites and, if possible, add an extra layer of security against rogue traders by using a credit card to make the purchase. And if you do buy from sites based abroad, find out about any extra shipping and duty costs.

It may also be worth having a look at second-hand resale sites such as www.tinytogs4u.co.uk or the Buy and Sell message forums found at parenting sites such as www.ukparents.co.uk.

expert view

There's a temptation to spend, spend, spend when there's a new baby on the way, says Catherine O'Dolan, editor of *Junior* magazine. Here are her tips for saving money. (For *Junior* subscription details, telephone 01858 438874 or visit **www.juniormagazine.co.uk**.)

CLOTHES:

* Buy quality, well-made clothes and they will last for several siblings and still look great. Cheaper clothes are often a false economy; the threads become loose, and they'll look rubbish after a few washes.

* Don't be afraid to splash out on a funky designer outfit for your baby (for yourself too, if it will boost post-birth confidence), but don't make the mistake of keeping it for best. Babies grow out of clothes quickly, so why not let her wear it at every opportunity? She'll be the talk of the NCT (National Childbirth Trust) get-togethers.

* Oh, and don't forget the BabyGap sale rails, where bargains are always to be had.

QUALITY TOY BRANDS:

* Adopt the same philosophy for buying children's toys: avoid the 'compatible with other leading brands' toys and go for the real McCoy (think Baby Lego). There are plenty of pretenders out there, but the quality brands are still the most enduring.

NAPPY LAUNDERING SERVICES:

* If you want to do your bit for the environment, then you'll want to use washable nappies. But who wants to be elbow-deep in pooey nappies?

The answer is to join a nappy laundering service, where dirty nappies are collected from your door in exchange for your next supply of pristine clean ones. Contact the National Association of Nappy Services (tel: 0121 693 4949, www.changeanappy.co.uk) for a list of services nationwide.

TRAVELLING EQUIPMENT:

* There are a couple of products that I'd strongly recommend. The first must-have is a baby sling. Small babies love the cosy closeness of being carried where they can feel your heartbeat and gentle breathing; a carrier is also much easier to transport than a pushchair. The best baby carrier on the market by miles is the BabyBjorn (about £50, www.babybjorn.com). The latest version of the classic BabyBjorn sling comes in oh-so-covetable soft black leather, so it should appeal to both parents.

* My second recommended buy is the Tripp-Trapp high-chair by Stokke (about £120, www.stokke.com). It's a state-of-the-art high-chair that 'grows' with your child (it is suitable from six months to 'adult'), designed to encourage perfect posture and comfort – and it's aesthetically pleasing to the eye.

PRIMARY RESOURCES

PARENTING MAGAZINES

Baby Magazine
tel: 020 7226 2222

Baby's Best Buys
tel: 01353 654430
www.wvip.co.uk

Junior
tel: 020 7761 8900
www.juniormagazine.co.uk

Mother and Baby
tel: 020 7874 0200
www.motherandbaby.co.uk

Natural Parent
tel: 020 8944 9555

New Baby
tel: 01353 654430
www.newbabymagazine.co.uk

Prima Baby
tel: 020 7519 5500
www.havingababy.co.uk

GENERAL PARENTING ADVICE SITES

www.babycentre.co.uk
www.babyworld.co.uk
www.bounty.com
www.e-parents.org
www.family2000.org.uk
www.ivillage.co.uk/pregnancyandbaby
www.mumsnet.com
www.planetoneparent.com
www.smallfolk.co.uk
www.tigerchild.com
http://magazine.urbia.co.uk

ONLINE RETAILERS

www.ababy.co.uk
www.b4baby.com
www.babiesrus.co.uk
www.babycare-direct.co.uk
www.babycentre.co.uk
www.babyjunction.co.uk
www.babymunchkins.com
www.babys-mart.co.uk
www.caringtouch.co.uk
www.discountbabystore.co.uk
www.gltc.co.uk
www.jojomamanbebe.co.uk
www.mamasandpapas.co.uk
www.nurserydirect.co.uk
www.nurserygoods.com
www.scallywagsbaby.com
www.smilechild.co.uk
www.thebabycatalogue.com
www.thetotalbabyshop.com
www.tinytogs4u.co.uk

HIGH-STREET RETAILERS

BabyGap
tel: 020 7437 0138
www.gap.com/babygap

Boots
tel: 0845 070 8090
www.wellbeing.com

Early Learning Centre
tel: 08705 352352
www.elc.co.uk

Mothercare
tel: 08453 304030
www.mothercare.co.uk

Tesco
tel: 0870 6076 060
www.tesco.com/babystore

beds

the basics

In bed we laugh, in bed we cry;
And, born in bed, in bed we die.
The near approach a bed may show
Of human bliss to human woe.

Isaac de Benserade (1612–1691), translated by Samuel Johnson

The importance of your bed cannot be overestimated. Along with the office chair, the seat to work and the armchair in front of the TV, there aren't many places you're going to be spending more time in your life. In fact, you can accurately state that a third of your life will be spent tucked up in bed. And as Isaac de Benserade presciently noted, some pretty significant life events will occur while you are in bed: birth, death ... you can fill in the rest. So buying the correct bed is up there with buying property and cars as one of life's key purchases.

With over four million sold each year, beds account for a £1 billion chunk of total furniture sales in the UK. You would, therefore, rightly expect the industry to be vigorously regulated for quality and price. Sadly, the bed industry seems to be more frontier town than civilized city when it comes to a mature and shared system for buyers to compare and contrast wares. What's more, retailers seem to persist with confusing buyers with jargon and fluctuating pricing.

By far the most popular type of bed purchased – about 35 per cent of the total – is the double divan, namely, a mattress on top of a deep-sided base. About a quarter of all beds sold are bedsteads –

mattresses placed on metal frames and slats. Others options include futons, bunk beds, sofa beds, adjustable beds and that seventies stalwart, the waterbed. But it is the quality of the mattress you buy that most determines whether you will sleep soundly for the next ten years – the recommended lifespan for beds as decreed by the Sleep Council.

do you even need a new bed?

Before making any purchase, though, you should first decide whether you really need a new bed. Are you suffering from sleeplessness? Are you waking in the morning with headaches and muscular pains? Do not automatically assume that your bed is to blame. Lifestyle and environmental influences are common causes of sleeplessness too. Noise, late-night drinking, excessive heat, stress are just a handful of known disturbers, but if you can answer yes to more than a couple of the following questions, then you should certainly consider getting a new bed:

* When lying in bed, do you feel springs and ridges beneath the mattress's surface?
* When moving in bed (make of this what you will), do you hear creaks and crunches?
* Do you and your partner roll together – unintentionally – when in bed?
* Would it be embarrassing if anyone were to see your bed without its covers?
* Is the bed older than ten years? (One made before 1986 will not meet the UK's fire safety regulations.)
* Is it a hand-me-down bed?

Still not convinced? If you're reluctant to give up on your beloved bed despite all its foibles, then consider how unhygienic it is likely to be after all these years. Your mattress will absorb up to a pint of your sweat each night and half a kilo of dead skin a year. And without near-fanatical vacuuming, your mattress will probably be home to millions of mites and other invisible little nasties.

choosing your bed

So now you're standing in the doorway of the local bed shop. What do you need to look for in a mattress? Well, first you need to know what's going on inside that bouncy rectangle. Some cheaper mattresses can be filled with synthetic padding or foam (although expensive foam beds are available), but you should never cut corners when buying a bed, so you would be well advised to seek out the best you can afford. This will invariably be a sprung mattress.

Most quality modern mattresses are filled with hundreds of steel pocket springs, so called because they are individually encased in a fabric pocket. The spring will be slightly compressed by its pocket and packed tightly with the others like a honeycomb. Wrapping the sprung centre will be a layer of coarse fibre, such as coir (coconut husk) or even horsehair. Next will be a layer of looser soft pads made of cotton, hair, wool, or a synthetic material. The final level of padding will be the main comfort layer, and will play a key role in allowing your body moisture to escape and deadening any noise from the moving springs. All the padding will be contained by the 'ticking' – the mattress's outermost layer of strong, tightly woven fabric. All of these materials will most likely be held together with tight stitching and 'tufting' – dozens of strong tapes threaded through the mattress and attached to washers. This is what gives quality mattresses their distinctive dimpled surface. Cheaper alternatives to tufting include quilting or diamond stitching.

the rest test

Clear yourself a day to test beds, as you don't want to be under the pressure of time. When testing a bed, there is simply no alternative to lying down on it and acting out some pretend sleep. Pressing the mattress with your hand or sitting on the edge and bouncing up and down a couple of times will not do. Professor Chris Idzikowski of the Sleep Assessment and Advisory Service says that you should ask the sales assistant whether you can try the bed for up to thirty minutes. Any decent shop should grant this wish.

Put aside any understandable embarrassment and rest on your

back and side – whatever your preferred sleeping position – for as long as you feel you need to assess the bed's comfort. Make sure you're not tired, as any bed will feel inviting (you don't actually want to doze off), and be sure to wear loose clothing and to take off your coat. The salesperson will invariably place a small mat under your feet to stop your shoes marking the bed, but it's best just to discard your shoes (no matter how antisocial that may be). Make sure that your partner accompanies you, too.

And think big. Disturbances from your partner are a common cause of sleeplessness (we toss and turn up to seventy times a night), so try a king-size bed (76 in. × 80 in.). Make sure, though, that you have the measurements of your bedroom and all access points before you go shopping.

To test whether you are getting the correct support, lie on your back and slide your hand into the hollow of your back. If your hand slides in easily, or there's a gap, the mattress is too firm for you. Likewise, if you can't slide your hand in, it's too soft. The mattress must mould to your shape and feel supportive, even when on your side. Contrary to popular belief, you should never actually sink into your bed.

In addition to rest testing, you will want answers to some important questions about the mattress:

* How many pocket springs does the mattress contain? Anything between three hundred and seven hundred is common. Generally, the more springs, the better the support, but you may find fewer springs more comfortable.

* What's the gauge of the springs? Heavy-gauge (thick) springs will offer a great deal of support, while light-gauge coils will give you less support. The higher the gauge number, the lighter the spring.

* How strong are the handles? It is recommended that you turn your mattress over and around every few months – every week in the first three months – to help keep its shape. If you buy a heavy mattress, it will need handles that can support its weight. Look for handles that are anchored to the springs and internal wiring. Next best are fabric handles that are sewn securely to the ticking. Avoid handles that are just clipped to the ticking with metal or plastic studs.

* Are the edges strong enough? When you sit down on the edge of the bed, you want it to hold your weight and not to sag. Quality beds will have strengthened edges to allow you to tie your shoelaces easily.

* How are the springs held together? Interconnecting wires keep the springs in place in the mattress. Too few and the springs can become misaligned.

* What material is the ticking made of? Polyester or cotton–polyester blends are the most common. You may see vinyl used, but this will stretch and sag over time and restrict your mattress from breathing. Better mattresses use damask. Some may contain silk, but this is largely a sales gimmick, as you are unlikely to ever feel the benefit by sleeping next to the mattress without a sheet. You will see 'pillow top' mattresses too, which have additional padding for your head, but you must decide when rest-testing whether this is really worth the extra expense.

* Is the bed long enough? If you are tall (over six foot), make sure the bed is at least six inches longer than your height. Many manufacturers will tailor the length to suit your needs, but standard shop sizes seem to go up to seven feet.

---

bed sizes

twin	=	39 in. × 75 in.
double	=	54 in. × 75 in.
queen	=	60 in. × 80 in.
king	=	76 in. × 80 in.

When considering the type of base to go with the mattress, it is best to try and make sure they are intended to go with one another. If you do find the perfect mattress, but prefer a base from another manufacturer, it is important to get the right size. Sizes are being standardized more and more, but not all manufacturers agree on what, for example, a king size means. The measurements shown here, though, are the most commonly adhered to.

Divans are probably the most practical bases, as they add extra support to the mattress as well as the option of drawers beneath your bed – always worth paying for if storage space is limited. Drawers don't affect the performance of the bed either, as they use the divan's 'dead space'. Think about the combined height of the mattress and divan, though. How easy will it be to get in and out of bed?

Bedsteads are also common, but it is imperative to make sure the slatted base will adequately support your mattress. A slatted base will improve ventilation and provide fewer places for allergens to accumulate, but the slats should be secured to the frame and evenly spaced, with the gaps between them no wider than the slats themselves (or the mattress's springs). The slats should also be constructed of a flexible, laminated material rather than wood or metal. A cheap bedstead and an expensive mattress is certainly a false economy. Remember too that you could invalidate a new mattress's guarantee by using an old base. Check the small print.

buying your bed

Price shouldn't really be a consideration when buying a bed: always get the best you can afford. In the UK, the average spend on a double divan is, according to the Sleep Council, £447 – far too low. A well sprung, quality bed is more likely to cost up to £1,000, but prices can go up to £10,000. Ask whether there is an option to pay by instalments. Many larger bed shops and department stores will offer interest-free credit. But beware being persuaded to try just one brand – the salesperson may stand to earn a financial reward for pushing that one brand in particular.

Possibly due to their price, beds often seem to be on near-permanent sale. Ask shops when their next sale is due and always try to haggle – bed prices always seem to be fluid. You may not get a reduction, but you might get free home delivery or an extended warranty. It is always worth checking if the delivery firm will also take your old bed away for free (local authorities have a collection scheme, but will probably charge for it), and whether they will assemble the bed rather than just ringing the doorbell, dumping it on your doorstep and driving off. Look out too for shops that offer to deliver a substitute should your model be out of stock. Insist that you require a no-substitute clause in your delivery terms. Check before you sign anything.

When it comes to your warranty, it is helpful to insist on a comfort guarantee, typically 30–60 days, in addition to any lifetime guarantee against defects. You can sleep soundly if you know that you have the option of returning the bed should it not live up to your expectations.

firm, medium, or soft?

The common perception is that the firmer the mattress, the better it is for your back. This is not necessarily the case. Your choice is further complicated by the fact that there is no industry standard for grading firmness.

Don't assume that if you have a bad back, you should automatically choose a bed with a label saying something like Posturepedic, Backcare Collection or Orthos. These terms simply mean that the beds are among the firmest in the manufacturers' range. Although firm beds can alleviate back pain, an overly firm bed may aggravate your condition. And some conditions may actually benefit from a softer bed, so ask your doctor or a specialist for advice, and try all ranges. Always check too that you are using the correct pillow, as a bad one could be the root cause of your pain.

If you and your partner have different needs, consider a zip-and-link bed – two single bases with separate mattress-types zipped together.

Don't let children bounce up and down on it though – especially the edges – or bend any internal wires or supports, as this will obviously invalidate any warranty. As will any stains, so use a protective sheet.

what about futons, sofa beds, bunk beds and waterbeds?

Futons and sofa beds are expressly designed for convenience – they're the ideal place for stopover friends to flop for the night. They should never be considered for your principal bed. If you need one for the spare room, or for space reasons, the same rules apply. Do not cut costs and always check the quality of the mattress first.

Bunk beds are another perfect solution to limited space, though as they invariably use slats to hold the mattress, you should give extra consideration to their quality. And because they're used by children, think safety. Are the safety bars strong and high enough? Is the ladder sturdy and non-slip? Is the mattress suitable for a growing child?

Waterbeds may seem a bit dated and the butt of frequent jokes, but they do claim to offer body support without any pressure points. They are hygienic, good for allergy sufferers, the pregnant and the bed-bound. Movement can be controlled, as can heat, but they will cost at least £1,000. Rest-test one, but look for dealers who are members of the British Waterbed Association.

PRIMARY RESOURCES

BED RETAILERS

Bed Company
tel: 0845 130 3339
www.bedcompany.co.uk

Bedcity
tel: 0800 092 0972
www.justclickbeds.com

Bensons for Beds
tel: 0808 044 0000
www.bensonsforbeds.co.uk

Dreams
tel: 01628 530800
www.dreamsplc.com

The Iron Bed Company
tel: 01243 578888
www.ironbed.com

Online Beds
tel: 01942 726251
www.onlinebeds.com

The Sleep Centre
tel: 01843 850850
www.thesleepcentre.co.uk

LEADING MANUFACTURERS

Dunlopillo
tel: 01423 872411
www.dunlopillo.co.uk

Hypnos
tel: 01844 348200
www.hypnos.ltd.uk

Layezee Beds
tel: 01924 421200
www.layezee.co.uk

Savoir Beds
tel: 020 8838 4838
www.savoirbeds.co.uk

Sealy UK
tel: 01697 320342
www.sealyuk.co.uk

Silentnight
tel: 01282 813051
www.silentnight.co.uk

Relyon
tel: 01823 667501
www.relyon

Slumberland
tel: 0161 628 4886
www.slumberland.co.uk

Vi-Spring
tel: 01752 366311
www.vispring.co.uk

(For full list of manufacturers visit
www.bedfed.org.uk/ordmemb.
cfm?sort=1)

DEPARTMENT STORES AND NATIONWIDE CHAINS THAT STOCK BEDS

Allders
tel: 0845 234 0139
www.allders.com

Debenhams
tel: 020 7408 4444
www.debenhams.com

Furniture Village (including the
London Bed Company)
tel: 020 7318 3807
www.furniturevillage.co.uk

House of Fraser
tel: 020 7529 4700
www.houseoffraser.co.uk

IKEA
tel: 020 8208 5600
www.ikea.co.uk

John Lewis
tel: 08456 049049
www.johnlewis.com

Mothercare (for children's
mattresses)
tel: 08453 304030
www.mothercare.com

Selfridges
tel: 020 7318 3456
www.selfridges.co.uk

NB: Always avoid buying
mattresses over the phone or via
the internet without trying them
out first.

BED INFORMATION

British Waterbed Association
tel: 0870 603 0202
www.waterbed.org

The National Bed Federation
tel: 020 7589 4888
www.bedfed.org.uk

The Sleep Assessment and
Advisory Service
tel: 02892 622266
www.neuronic.com/sleep.htm

The Sleep Council
tel: 01756 791089
www.sleepcouncil.org.uk

bicycles

the basics

It's the same every year: we catch a few hours of the Tour de France on TV and all of a sudden we think we're Lance Armstrong. Off we go (in the car, no doubt) to the nearest bike shop with the intention of making a life-changing purchase that will help us get fit and beat the traffic at the same time. But a few weeks later, the bike has joined its cousin, the exercise bike, behind cardboard boxes in the garage and those tight Lycra shorts have, thank God, been pushed to the back of a drawer. The lesson is clear: don't buy a bike on a whim. Spend some time researching what you need and you might end up actually testing those shiny, new mudguards.

The range available to you is enormous. Gone are the days when your choice was limited to boneshakers with baskets or a five-gear road racer with go-fast stripes attached to the spokes. The evolution of bicycles over the last few decades has seen us sitting upon all manner of contraptions – Choppers, BMXs, mountain bikes – but the good news for the consumer is that after years of technological experimentation and design, the bicycle market is mature and offers plenty of value for money.

So what do you want to use your bike for? Your answer will largely determine what type of bike you buy. Do you just want it for the occasional Sunday afternoon pootle by the canal? Have you had it with public transport and decided to beat the traffic with pedal power? Are you looking to use a bike for exercise? Are you planning a cycling holiday? Each of these scenarios is suited to different types of bikes and to different configurations of tyre types, gears, handlebars and frames.

Most bike shops will typically offer you the following range:

- *road bikes:* The classic bicycle design, with drop handlebars and thin tyres.
- *mountain bikes:* The most popular choice, due to their comfortable handling, upright seating, strength and versatility. About 70 per cent of all bicycle sales are now mountain bikes, even though the highest climb most of them will see is from the road to the pavement.
- *hybrids:* As their name suggests, hybrids are a cross between road and mountain bikes. They have narrower tyres and are sleeker than mountain bikes, and are thus ideal for commuting.
- *comfort bikes:* The best choice for the weekend leisure rider, due to their softer saddles, lower gearing and more upright riding position.
- *kids' bikes:* Many are just smaller versions of adult bikes, but most shops offer one-gear bikes for the younger child.
- *niche bikes:* Everyone knows about tandems, but 'recumbents' are gaining in popularity. These allow the rider to pedal in a low reclining position and boast better comfort for long-distance riding because they reduce the pressure points on your seat and back.

making your purchase

When you head off to buy a bike, look for a dedicated bike shop rather than a shop that happens to offer half a dozen or so models, such as a supermarket. The quality of service and knowledge will be much higher, and you should especially look out for bike shops that are Association of Cycle Traders (ACT) members. There's a good chance, too, that some of the staff will be CyTech-accredited, a national level of competence for mechanics accepted by all the major cycling organizations in the UK.

Bike shops should also offer the best post-sales service and will usually give your bike a free tune-up a few months after you have bought it to make sure it is still set up correctly. And note that buying by phone or the internet should only be considered when you have already worked out the exact model and specifications, but more importantly tried it out beforehand.

The best time to find bargains is usually in the autumn when shops are looking to make room for next year's new stock and the summer rush for bikes has slowed. January and February are usually a good time too.

And try to buy everything you need together. There are a few essential accessories that you will require and it's best to buy them at the same time as you get the bike so that you can try to get a better deal.

road-testing a bicycle

Once you have spoken to someone in the shop about which type of bike is right for your needs, you will need to try a few out. This doesn't mean ringing the bell and kicking the tyres a few times; this means taking the bike out for a spin. Make sure, though, that you familiarize yourself with the bike's specifications beforehand, so you know exactly what you are testing and comparing.

Begin by taking each bike out on the road for five minutes or so. (You may have to leave something like a driving licence as security.) Really put it through its paces. Ride up a hill using the full range of gears to see if they shift smoothly. Brake hard to test how responsive the brakes are. Make lots of sharp turns. Assess how comfortable the saddle is.

Back at the shop, look for any 'wheel wobble' by keeping your eye on the brake pads when the wheel is moving. If there are wobbles, it means the wheel is off-balance and needs to be fixed. The brake pads should also be exactly parallel to the wheel's rim. If they're not, the brakes will wear down unevenly. The bike's 'bearings' – the wheel hubs, the handlebar stem and the pedals – should not be too loose or too stiff. And check to see whether the brake-cable wires are finished tidily with little metal caps.

finding the right size

For men, the best way to check whether a bike is the right size is to straddle the crossbar while wearing the shoes you are likely to be riding in and to measure the distance between your crotch and the crossbar. For a mountain bike, the distance should be about four inches (10 cm). For a road racer, the distance should be about two inches (5 cm). For a women's bike, which will typically have a frame without a crossbar, you should use the same test by gauging where a crossbar would be.

As well as height, you need to check the bike's reach – the distance of the handlebars from your body. You'll have your own idea of what distance is comfortable here, but a quick test is to see if you can see the front wheel's hub over the handlebars. If you can, the reach may be too small for you. You also want your elbows to be slightly bent, but don't forget that the handlebar and saddle heights can be adjusted. Ask a sales assistant to adjust them if you think it will help.

frames

When considering which frame to opt for, the most important factor is the construction material. There are four realistic options, namely steel, aluminium, titanium and graphite. Each has its own pros and cons, but look for the frame's 'decal', which will tell you what brand, type and standard of material has been used. You will find this on the tube under the saddle or on the down tube beneath.

Steel is the traditional construction material for frames, but is increasingly being surpassed by newer, modern alternatives. Its durability and strength are its plus points, but the fact that it is heavy and vulnerable to rust means that it tends to only be used on entry-level bikes nowadays. However, steel is popular for forks (the long brackets that attach the wheels to the frame), because of its strength and because it absorbs shock well. Don't forget, though, that there are some high-quality steel alloys to look out for. Chrome molybdenum is perhaps the best known and is usually referred to as 'chromoly' or 'chrome-moly'.

Aluminium is now perhaps the most popular material for constructing frames. Since the 1980s, when manufacturers developed ways to make viable aluminium tubing for bikes, it has been favoured for its lightness, strength and shock absorbance. Pure aluminium is not strong enough to use for bikes, so look out for which aluminium alloy is being offered. Two popular alloys are 6061 and 7005. These numbers indicate the levels of magnesium, silicon and zinc that have been added to the aluminium, but, without being too technical, all you need to know is that most manufacturers believe 6061 aluminium to be superior, because it is easy to manipulate under heat and thus better for adding strength-increasing features such as butting and tapered walls.

Titanium, or 'ti', is the most expensive frame material available. It offers many of the same advantages as aluminium, and many experienced riders value its springiness and superior handling. Aluminium and vanadium are mixed with titanium to make the alloy used in bikes, so look out for the alloy grade.

The two most common types are 3Al/2.5V and 6Al/4V, and, as their names suggest, the grades indicate the blend of the alloy; 6Al/4V is considered to be the best alloy because it is harder and lighter, but both grades are extremely good materials for a frame.

Graphite (carbon) frames are unique, because they are not actually made of metal. Instead, a fabric is impregnated with resin and then shaped. It allows for new designs and shapes, and, like steel, is a popular material for forks. It is also expensive.

wheels and tyres

The weight of the wheel is just as important as the weight of the frame. The 'wheel feel' alters dramatically according to weight, because it is a rotating object. Just a few grams' difference will noticeably alter the wheel's handling, acceleration and climbing ease.

Obviously, the construction material of the wheel will affect its weight – again, aluminium is very popular – but performance is also affected by the number of spokes and the type of rim.

The traditional number of spokes for a wheel is thirty-two, but some modern bikes have reduced this number to cut down wind drag. This is only really worth it if you are serious about your cycling and plan on adding the odd yellow jersey to your wardrobe.

You have two choices when it comes to rims – the strip of metal that joins the spokes to the tyres. Box-section rims are square-shaped and offer better comfort for leisure riders. Speed freaks should opt for aero-section rims, which are triangular. They give a harder ride than box-section rims, but are more aerodynamic.

Tyre sizes are largely determined by the weight of the rider and the required use of the bike. Most racer tyres meet the European '700c' standard, namely, that the tyre's outside diameter is 700 mm. The sizes then break down according to the tyre's width:

---

tyre sizes

700×20: Ideal for professional cyclists, speedsters and light riders.

700×23: Good for most conditions, but best for racing and training.

700×25: Long-lasting and good for shock absorption.

700×28: Tough, and thus ideal for commuting, touring and heavy riders.

You may want to consider Kevlar-belted tyres if you are going to use your bike in town. These have a layer of Kevlar – a strong, light, synthetic fibre – under the tread surface to cut the risk of a puncture, but they are more expensive. Don't confuse them with Kevlar-beaded tyres – used by competitive cyclists to save the minimal weight of steel beads (the hoops at either side of the tyre). Most tyres will last between one and two thousand miles depending on your weight and riding style, and whether they are used on the front or back wheel.

gears

The more the merrier is the popular perception, but you need to ask yourself (and the sales assistant) whether you really need the thirty gears commonly offered on bikes today. After all, you will be paying for them. Most leisure riders would be more than happy with twenty, but if you anticipate plenty of climbs ahead of you, more gears are certainly an advantage. You can work out the number of gears on a bike by multiplying the number of chain rings (the sprockets near the pedals) by the number of cassette cogs (the sprocket on the rear wheel).

accessories

Before you leave the shop, don't forget to purchase some key accessories (it's unlikely the sales assistant will let you do so even if you forget). Obviously, you need a helmet. By and large, it's a matter of comfort and style, as helmets must now meet safety regulations. It's also worth considering riding gloves for extra grip, a water bottle and holder, a decent puncture kit, some lights, a quality lock and a pump. You should be able to do a deal if you buy all these together with the bike in one transaction, so ask.

kids' bikes

Never be tempted to buy a bike that a child will grow into. A child is likely to have more accidents if it struggles to handle an oversized bike. It's also not wise to give a child under eight a bike with conventional hand brakes. Get them a bike with stabilizers and foot brakes. And don't give a child under ten a bike with more than one gear.

Check the number of spokes, too. Most children's bikes have twenty-eight spokes, but cheaper models may have twenty or so, which will offer less strength. Pedals must offer good grip, so avoid those slippery plastic things. Metal pedals are better, but not ones with sharp metal teeth.

insurance

Bicycle theft is a huge problem, particularly in urban areas. Your best defence is to buy decent insurance, one that offers new-for-old, public liability, worldwide cover, no claims bonuses and personal accident cover. Your best bet is probably to become a member of the Cyclists' Touring Club (CTC – see 'primary resources'), which will

only for the brave

Criminals operate rackets in which they steal bikes from college towns like Oxford and Cambridge, then sell them on among legitimate bikes at, for example, popular street markets – or so says urban legend. Remember this if you are ever tempted to buy a bike second-hand 'from the street' or through the classifieds in *Loot*, for example. Ask the seller if they can provide the bike's receipts and unique code.

Police auctions are another way of sourcing cheap bikes. Retrieved stolen bikes whose owners fail to claim them are auctioned off to the public. Cambridge Police (tel: 01223 358966, www.cambs.police.uk) hold quarterly sales, and the Metropolitan Police auctions off its lost property via www.frankgbowen.co.uk. Check with your local police force or www.auctions.co.uk for other nationwide police auctions.

expert view

Richard Hallett, the technical editor of *Cycling Weekly* magazine, recommends that you remember the following points:

* Mountain bikes are highly versatile, so one of these or the more road-oriented hybrid bikes makes a good starting point. But forget full suspension unless you fancy some serious off-road adventure.

* Look for a rigid fork if that Sustrans route (the national network of cycle paths) is the most demanding surface you will tackle.

* For road use, get your dealer to replace knobbly, mountain-bike tyres with fat, slick 'city' tyres which roll more easily.

* Drop-handlebar-equipped road bikes are faster and more efficient, but require careful handling on poorly maintained roads. They also need more careful setting-up for a comfortable riding position. Look for a dealer with access to 'Bio Racer', or a similar positioning system to make the process easier.

* Don't forget mudguards – a common mistake. They are virtually essential for the regular cycle commuter.

* Even leisure cyclists benefit from clipless pedals and cycling shoes such as Shimano's SPD system, which have an exit action that is easy to learn. Shoes with a walking sole and a clipless retention device offer the best of both worlds and dramatically improve pedalling efficiency.

* Carry at least two spare tubes, tyre levers and a pump, and learn to use them.

give you free public liability insurance. Membership costs £27, or £10 for those under twenty-six. In addition to the insurance cover, you will receive a magazine, advice on cycling routes, discounts at shops and access to their rescue service. The British Cycling Federation, a more sports-oriented organization, also offer free public liability insurance as part of their membership, but with both organizations you will have to get a quote for new-for-old cover. This will be calculated according to the value of your bike.

All insurance will be conditional on your recording the bike's unique frame number, which you should also report to the police if making a crime report. For added peace of mind, it's a good idea to register your frame number with **www.bikeregister.com**, too.

ethics watch

When *Ethical Consumer* magazine examined bicycle manufacturers, one point of concern was workers' rights. Most imported bikes sold in the UK came from Taiwan, which has attracted criticism on labour rights and environmental protection issues. Taiwanese companies also commonly subcontract manufacture to even lower-wage economies in the region.

One of the cycle brands attracting most attention was Land Rover – licensed from the Ford Motor Co. Ford has been criticized for lobbying for more road-building and for promoting even greater trade with China, a country still criticized for its human rights record.

The magazine's advice was to choose locally made products. Overall best buys were Pashley, Dawes and Brompton brands labelled as manufactured in the UK. Sterling Resources (Universal Bikes) also scored well on workers' rights. All bicycles were, of course, best buys for environmental impact reasons. For more information, visit www.ethicalconsumer.org or call 0161 226 2929.

PRIMARY RESOURCES

CYCLING ORGANIZATIONS

British Cycling Federation
tel: 0161 274 2010
www.bcf.uk.com

Cyclists' Touring Club
tel: 01483 417217
www.ctc.org.uk

The National Cycle Network
tel: 0117 929 0888
www.sustrans.co.uk and
www.saferoutestoschools.org.uk

CYCLING MAGAZINES

Cycle Sport
tel: 020 8774 0600
www.cycle-sport.com

Cycling Plus
tel: 01458 271111
www.cyclingplus.co.uk

Cycling Weekly
tel: 020 8774 0600
www.cyclingweekly.com

Mountain Bike Rider
tel: 020 8774 0600
www.mountainbikerider.co.uk

Mountain Bike UK
tel: 01225 442244
www.mbuk.com

ProCycling
tel: 01795 414892
www.procycling.com

Velo Vision
tel: 01904 438224
www.velovision.co.uk

CYCLE SHOP ONLINE LOCATORS

www.bikemagic.com
www.bikinguk.net/dealers
www.cycleweb.co.uk
www.handbooks.co.uk/bikesindex.htm
www.hikerbiker.co.uk/bikeshop

ONLINE BIKE SHOPS

www.bicyclenet.co.uk
www.cyclestore.co.uk
www.halfords.com
www.ukbikestore.co.uk

RETAIL TRADE ASSOCIATION

Association of Cycle Traders
tel: 01892 526081
www.cyclesource.co.uk

MANUFACTURERS

For a full list, look online at:
www.bikinguk.net/manufacturers
or:
http://uk.dir.yahoo.com/business_
and_economy/shopping_and_
services/sport/cycling/gear_and_
equipment/makers

cameras

the basics

Due to rapid technological developments in the camera market over the last decade, including the introduction of two major new formats, the consumer must now make dozens of daunting decisions about which features they require on the 400 plus cameras on offer. But before you start deciding whether you really need TTL flash metering, you have to establish, as ever, exactly what you want the camera for. Are you planning to take the odd holiday snap a few times a year? Are you looking to join an amateur photography club? Or do you want a digital camera so that you can email photos of that Amsterdam minibreak to friends?

Most people normally make do with the 'point-and-shoot' compact cameras that have been the mainstay of the market for the last fifteen years or so. But in the last couple of years and amid much industry hype, sales of digital cameras have exploded and they are now the market's runaway growth sector. In addition to this, some of the major camera manufacturers got together in the mid-1990s to launch the Advanced Photo System (APS), which claims to offer a much easier experience for the average photographer than traditional 35 mm cameras.

So, when you go into most camera shops today, you will typically be presented with a choice of four camera types – the compact, the digital, 35 mm SLRs (Single Lens Reflex) or APS. Of course, more options exist for the professional photographer, but unless you're planning on spending over £1,000, you're best advised to stick to these main types.

compacts / point-and-shoots

Sometimes mockingly called PHDs (Push Here Dummy), compact cameras are understandably popular. Their small size makes them extremely practical for casual use, such as holidays and drink-fuelled nights out – there's none of that fiddling around with aperture size and large lenses. But they offer other advantages too.

Unlike APS and digital cameras, you can use any old 35 mm film with a compact. This has distinct advantages, particularly when you find yourself stuck without film on that dusty trail in the middle of nowhere. The nearest shop, if it has any film at all, is only ever likely to have 35 mm in stock. Most compacts also have a built-in flash, which is always handy, and their convenient weight and size make them perfect for keeping in pockets and handbags.

However, there are some downsides to remember and some key features to look for with compacts. To start with, that handy little flash is likely to be of poor quality. You'll be lucky, in fact, if it manages to illuminate anything beyond ten to fifteen feet, even with 400ASA film. The lens is unlikely to be of the same quality that you would get with an SLR either (you shouldn't really get enlargements over 5 in. × 7 in. with a compact), but perhaps the most limiting aspect of compacts is that you have little, if any, control over the outcome of the picture. You push the button, and it does the rest.

Don't be taken in by lots of snazzy features. With compacts, it is often better to opt for slightly cheaper models with fewer features than more expensive ones that boast all the latest show-off gizmos. The standard features that you should look for are a zoom lens of no more than a 35 to 100 mm range of magnification (38–140 mm 'superzooms' rarely offer any real optical quality), a flash that allows red-eye reduction, and a solid, sturdy construction. You shouldn't really need to pay much more than £200 to achieve this, but anything beneath £100 and picture quality will decrease rapidly. And as with all cameras, the larger and clearer the viewfinder, the better.

35 mm SLRs

Many photographers believe SLR cameras to be the most versatile on the market today for the average user. Most SLRs allow the user to switch quickly between lenses and between manual and automatic control, and they are the cheapest way for someone to get into serious amateur photography.

As the basic mechanics haven't changed much over the years, it is worth thinking about buying one that's second-hand instead of plumping straight-away for a modern one packed full of electronic gadgetry that will fail quicker over time.

The feature that you want to ensure is of the best quality, whether it's second-hand or new, is the lens. The range of SLR lenses available can seem overwhelming, because you can get manual focus (MF) as well as automatic focus (AF) lenses, but you will want something like a 28–105 mm Sigma lens as your minimum standard.

Also, with SLRs, you can detach the lens, which allows you to shop around for camera bodies and lenses separately. You must, however, remember to make sure that the lens is available in the same mount size as the camera you are considering or already own. (A good tip is to settle on one mount size for life, then even if you upgrade later, your older equipment will all be interchangeable. Many manufacturers intentionally offer different mount sizes, so check carefully.)

If you are buying a SLR to help you learn how to use a camera, think twice before buying an expensive AF lens. Even though they offer the convenience of a Point-and-Shoot, an AF lens does not always produce the same quality picture offered by an MF. Their 'ease of use' will also encourage you to take far more photographs. Learn how to use an MF lens and not only will you will save on film (is there really any need for fourteen photos of that Spanish sunset?), you will be buying a cheaper camera, because MF lenses lack the fancy electronics an AF lens needs and are therefore cheaper and more reliable. In the process, you will also be forced to learn how to operate the camera's focus and exposure, which will always lead to better photos.

When it comes to the construction material of the camera body, look for metal over plastic. Cameras typically take a fair battering over their lives, and you want to be able to protect your film and delicate lenses.

Overall, you should be able to get a quality starter SLR for under £400, but always shop around, particularly online, once you have settled on the make and model.

APS

The Advanced Photo System (APS) was launched in 1996 by a group of leading manufacturers. The system does away with 35 mm film and replaces it with a much smaller cartridge, allowing for some tiny compact APS models. The cartridge allows much more flexibility than 35 mm, in that you can add information to each photograph such as the time, date and location of where it was taken. You can choose the size of the print format, too: the classic 6 in. × 4 in., the high-definition TV (HDTV) 7 in. × 4 in., or the panoramic 10 in. × 4 in. What's more, you can change the print format later.

The cartridges are very easy to load (unlike fiddly 35 mm film), and some let you swap cartridges around at any time without wasting film. On the negative side, however, black and white APS film is sometimes hard to find. Cartridge and printing costs are also higher than for 35 mm film, and many photographers claim that under close inspection, 35 mm cameras still offer greater sharpness and clarity than APS cameras.

A good APS compact will set you back between £150 and £200, but expensive Single Lens Reflex APS cameras are also available.

digital cameras

At first sight, digital cameras seem to be the perfect choice – no film costs, no developing costs if you use a printer, and they let you assess (and discard) your images immediately. These are undeniable advantages, but most camera experts will unite in saying that entry-level digital cameras still do not offer the amateur photographer much in the way of flexibility and control unless you are prepared to spend thousands of pounds. Their conclusion is that digital cameras are only really worth buying if you just want to use them for basic holiday and home snaps that you intend to use for emailing on to others, building websites or manipulating images on a computer. Conventional cameras, in other words, still provide much better quality images.

The lens quality of digital cameras under £1,000 still can't match a cheaper SLR, for example, and even though there have been large strides in recent years with the quality of resolution (2-megapixel resolution is now the norm on low-end models), a half-decent flatbed scanner – extremely cheap nowadays – will still deliver better-quality images when scanning from a 35 mm print than most digital cameras can produce.

Storage of images is another problem presented by digital cameras. While you may wish to end the habit of storing hundreds of

ethics watch

As with all technical goods, says *Ethical Consumer* magazine, obsolescence is a consideration for camera customers who want a lasting product that is repairable or upgradeable. Only analogue SLRs can really be said to offer that facility.

Most cameras need batteries, even just to power the flash, but digital cameras use up by far the greatest amount of battery power, and not all models come with rechargeable batteries or mains adapters. However, digital cameras produce less waste in that there are no chemicals or gelatine film needed to produce pictures, and selective print-out means that there are no wasted shots.

The producers of digital cameras are a cross section of traditional camera-making companies and computer equipment giants who all saw the potential of increasing brand identity across both the camera and the PC peripherals platform. About three quarters of the popular brands have some link to the arms industry.

The optics companies supply the military with photographic, visibility, and imaging equipment, while the larger companies in the electronics industry supply just about anything. The scale of opportunities for such manufacturers is huge: Eastman Kodak has had hundreds of millions of dollars' worth of military contracts in the last decade. The

company has also been fined $1 million for failing to report a pollution incident and for unlawful behaviour relating to hazardous waste disposal. Kodak's Rochester New York plant has been at the centre of a debate about the emission of recognizable carcinogens.

The following companies display a mature approach to environmental reporting, and are therefore recommended as best buys: Casio, Fuji, Konica and Ricoh. For more information, visit www.ethicalconsumer.org or call 0161 226 2929.

prints in shoeboxes under the bed, you will now have to store your images on a computer disk, CD-ROM or hard drive instead. Is that really any more convenient? And what happens when you get a new computer? When you consider that most images are between 500 KB and 1 MB in size, then you can see how your meagre home computer can soon get full. If you want your grandchildren to be viewing your photos decades from now, digital cameras do not seem to be the answer.

Most digital cameras, although relatively easy to operate, also demand a certain level of familiarity with computers, especially if you want to manipulate an image. Are you sure you are up to it?

And don't forget you will have to pay for expensive memory cards – CompactFlash, SmartMedia and Sony's Memory Stick are the most common – instead of film. Digital cameras also have a habit of draining expensive batteries.

If you do decide that a digital camera is right for you, then look out for goodies such as a 'free' version of a design software package (a stripped down version of Adobe Photoshop is ideal) as part of the deal. Register, too, with photo-sharing websites such as **www.ofoto.com** to help limit the amount of storage space you use on your computer and to allow you to 'develop' pictures into conventional print formats if you wish.

As with all cameras, try the grip before buying to see how sturdy and secure it seems. And for better quality images go for a 3x optical zoom lens rather than digital zoom.

expert view

Neil Whitford, editor of *Which Camera?*, recommends you remember the following advice when shopping for cameras:

Digital cameras are the buzz product of the moment and the quantity sold looks set to exceed conventional cameras in the very near future. Many users, however, end up disappointed with their digital purchase or, conversely, spend over the odds for the specification they require.

The disappointment comes with the conviction that once a digital camera has been bought, there is no more outlay required – no more film or processing to pay for. While this may be true, digital photography does still require investment – batteries and digital memory cards will be first on the list of priorities, and if you want to produce your own prints at home, then special paper and inks for your printer will cost you dearly.

It is in the initial investment, however, that most buyers come unstuck. The belief with digital is that the more pixels your camera has the better the pictures will be. Not so. A finite number of pixels are required to produce a print of a given size. If your camera gathers more data than is needed, then some of it simply won't be used, and you may have paid for a 3- or even 4-megapixel camera when a 2-megapixel camera would suffice.

If your requirement is to produce ordinary-sized snapshots, view pictures on a computer screen or email them, look in the bottom third of the digital camera market. Here you will find some amazing bargains from companies such as Fujifilm and Olympus that have more than adequate specifications for most users' needs and, with smaller digital file sizes to deal with, are more cost-efficient in terms of both batteries and digital storage space.

Don't just stick to the best-known camera brands, either – whichever format you are buying. While makers such as Canon, Olympus and Nikon have a long heritage in the photographic world, you should know that they subcontract the manufacture of their cameras to the same factories that also produce cameras for some of the lesser-known brands. These can often offer comparable features, build qualities and guarantees for a lower price.

PRIMARY RESOURCES

CAMERA MAGAZINES

Amateur Photographer
tel: 020 7261 5100
www.amateurphotographer.com

British Journal of Photography
tel: 020 7306 7000
www.bjphoto.co.uk

What Camera
tel: 020 7261 5266
www.whatcamera.co.uk

What Digital Camera
tel: 020 7451 0970
www.what-digital-camera.com

Which Camera?
tel: 01799 544200
www.whichcamera.co.uk

ONLINE RETAILERS

www.apsdirect.co.uk
www.bestcameras.co.uk
www.buyacamera.co.uk
www.camera-x-change.co.uk
www.cameras.co.uk
www.camerasdirect.co.uk
www.collegecameras.co.uk
www.fotofirst.co.uk
www.internetcamerasdirect.co.uk
www.jessops.com
www.mrcad.co.uk
www.sherwoods-photo.com
www.1tripcamera.com

CAMERA AND COMPONENT MANUFACTURERS

Agfa
tel: 0845 601 4563
www.agfa.co.uk

Canon
tel: 01737 220000
www.canon.co.uk

Casio
tel: 020 8450 9131
www.casio.co.uk

Epson
tel: 0800 220546
www.epson.co.uk

Fuji
tel: 020 7586 1477
www.fujifilm.co.uk

hp (formerly Hewlett Packard)
tel: 0870 241 1485
www.hp.com/uk

Jenoptik
www.jenoptik.com

JVC
www.jvc.co.uk

Kodak
tel: 0870 243 0270
www.kodak.co.uk

Konica
tel: 020 8751 6121
www.konica.co.uk

Kyocera
tel: 0118 931 1500
www.kyocera.co.uk

Leica
tel: 01908 246300
www.leica-camera.com

Minolta
tel: 01908 200400
www.minolta.co.uk

Minox
www.minox-web.de

Mustek
www.mustek-europe.com

Nikon
tel: 0800 230220
www.nikon.co.uk

Olympus
tel: 020 7253 2772
www.olympus.co.uk

Panasonic
tel: 01344 476540
www.panasonic.co.uk

Pentax
tel: 01753 792792
www.pentax.co.uk

Ricoh
tel: 01782 753300
www.ricoh.co.uk

Samsung
tel: 01952 292262
www.samsungelectronics.co.uk

Sanyo
tel: 01923 246363
www.sanyo.co.uk

Sony
tel: 08705 111999
www.sony.co.uk

Toshiba
tel: 01932 828828
www.toshiba.co.uk

Vivitar
tel: 01793 526211
www.vivitar.co.uk

PHOTO-STORING WEBSITES

www.ofoto.com
http://photos.yahoo.com

cars

the basics

Estate agents, traffic wardens, lawyers, tax collectors: if you were looking to complete the set, most people would not take long before coming up with the car salesman. Much maligned, justifiably in many cases, this particular species has a fierce reputation for inflicting pain and anxiety on its prey, but thankfully many alternatives now exist for the car-buying public. What's more, many buyers are now arming themselves with so much information that in some cases, they are more than a match for that man in the cheap suit smirking at you from underneath the showroom bunting.

As ever, it all begins with some basic decision-making. What do you need a car for? What are your transport requirements? How do you plan to pay for it? How long will it be before you are likely to need a newer model? How much can you spend on insurance? How much room have you got for parking? Should we collectively as a nation put so much trust in the opinion of Jeremy Clarkson? The answers to any of these questions could dramatically alter the type of car you end up trying to buy, but crucially you must have answered them before you set off on any test drives.

before you buy

When you have a good idea of the type of car you want to buy, get going on your homework as soon as possible. Thankfully, you now have the internet on your side, as well as the myriad dedicated magazines such as the *Glass's* price guides and *Autotrader*, so with just a few clicks on some of the more reliable car-buying websites you will soon establish a good ballpark figure for the price you should expect to pay for that class or particular model. It's worth visiting the Car Price Index website, too. It is a joint project between the Alliance & Leicester and *What Car?* magazine, and enables visitors to gauge whether prices, by class, are going up or down on a monthly basis compared to the same month a year before.

In addition, remember these following points:

* Never reveal how you intend to pay until you've discussed a price. Many dealers will kick off with the classic 'How much can you afford to pay each month?' You will severely weaken your hand if you let them know, especially if you are considering a finance or leasing option. If you want to fudge the issue, just say you are thinking of paying cash. What's a little white lie between fiends?

* Sell your old car yourself beforehand, rather than trade it in. Trade-in deals are rarely value for money. Again, the dealer will ask about this early on, so avoid answering, as it will affect their quote. A common sales tactic is to give you a seemingly low quote for the new car, but to make the money back by giving you a low trade-in price in return. If possible, sell the car via the classifieds in a magazine like *Autotrader* first.

* Always consider a car's resale value. Most people change cars every few years, so part of your homework should be to investigate the second-hand market of your preferred model. Cars famously lose value as soon as they are driven off the forecourt. Features that always help to preserve price are engine size, colour, the model's perceived image, the number of doors and 'luxuries' such as power steering, air conditioning and ABS brakes. The best advice is to be safe and go for averages. Go for a safe colour like red, black or a metallic look – avoid gold, yellow and white – and you could help shore up the price by a few per cent. Stick to mid-range models and mid-range engine sizes and always go for five-door over three-door models. Ideally, buy a model that includes as standard the said 'luxury' features, because paying extra for them will always prove to be less value. And get as many

safety features as you can afford. They retain value as well as retaining lives.

⊛ Timing is key. The hour, the day and the month you buy can all influence the chance of getting a bargain. The best time of year to buy a car is around Christmas, when people's bank accounts are otherwise occupied and forecourt business is therefore slow. The best day of the week to enter a car showroom is a Tuesday, because it's likely to be the least busy (weekends and Mondays are traditionally the busiest days) and hence the sales staff are more desperate to make a sale. Remember that most dealers operate a monthly bonus system for their sales staff, so go shopping in the very last days of the calendar month when the staff may be getting twitchy to reach their sales target. And don't try shopping when it's dark. Ideally, you want bright, sunny weather to let you see the car in detail. It helps too if it's really cold, so you can test whether the car's engine is up to those cold, early-morning starts (particularly important for second-hand cars).

⊛ Take a friend. Beyond the obvious safety concerns of test-driving a car with a complete stranger, a friend can act as a foil when it comes to bargaining. Just as sales staff will often adopt the good-cop, bad-cop routine with their manager, you can both agree on a similar counter-strategy. It helps to take some of the pressure off you if you can get your friend to take the hard line with the price. A friend can also stop you being drawn in by the patter of a good salesman.

⊛ Don't forget your overall costs. In addition to the price you end up paying for a car, you have to factor all the other extra costs into the equation, such as the insurance, the model's road tax, the expense of services, the petrol costs, breakdown cover and parking costs. Research all of these costs in advance.

financing the deal

You could write an entire book – people have – on the pitfalls of raising the money for your dream car. Best, of course, is just to turn up with a wad of £50 notes and, Arthur Daley style, hand over a bundle or two. Sadly, this only seems to happen on TV, so in most cases you will have to organize a loan with a bank or dealer. Alternatively, you can now lease a car.

The cheapest way to raise the money is to add the amount to your mortgage, if that's possible, but even getting a normal bank loan is preferable to agreeing to a finance package with a car dealer.

Whichever route you take, clearly establish in your head first what your maximum monthly limit is for repaying any loan. But beware the salesman who, with a nifty finger dance on a calculator, manages to present an agreeable monthly figure. After all, any loan period can be stretched out to make the monthly total seem smaller, but in the end you will always end up paying more. An optimum period to pay back the loan should be about three years. Any more than this and the dealer will be making an ever better return. Remember that the terms of a finance deal can be just as lucrative to the dealer as the price of the car itself.

If you aren't bringing your own money to the deal, you will have to take up one of three options presented by the dealers – hire purchase (HP), personal contract plans (PCPs) or leasing. All of them have their good and bad points, but all will be more costly than a previously organized loan with a bank or building society. Of course, the reason why they are offered in the first place is because many people don't qualify for secured loans or because they want the convenience of a one-stop solution.

hire purchase

Just the same as if you were buying a TV or kitchen on HP, you pay an initial deposit then monthly payments over a set period. The car will not be legally yours until the last payment. This is your best option if you are going to keep the car for a long time.

PCPs

The advantage of PCPs is that you pay a smaller deposit than HP and the monthly payments will be lower. But to own the car outright, you must make a much larger pre-arranged final payment. Alternatively, you can start another PCP (you will still not 'own' the car, though) or just hand the car back and walk away, in effect treating the whole deal as one long rental period. However, you will have to agree a maximum mileage limit, which will cost you dear if you exceed it.

leasing

Increasingly popular, leasing is similar to renting the car for a few years. All you have to worry about is filling her up with petrol and not exceeding an agreed maximum mileage limit. No servicing, tax or deposit to worry about. Of course, you have to weigh up the convenience against the fact that you will have nothing to show at the end of the lease period, as the car will return to the dealer, but leasing is often the only way many of us will be able to get behind the wheel of our fantasy car. You will normally have the option of buying the car, but always carefully consider what the depreciation is first and whether it is really good value for money. Be aware, too, that if you are forced to end the lease agreement early (because of theft or an accident, for example), you will be liable to a hefty release fee.

Whichever option you go for, carefully compare and contrast all the total final outgoings of each deal available to you. Never be drawn in by appealing monthly payment quotes. It is best, too, to ignore extended warranties and payment protection insurance. Both are very lucrative to the dealer, and extended warranties rarely offer better value over time than you would get from just taking the car to a local mechanic.

It is also worth noting that in any deal where there's a chance you will have to hand the car back at the end of the agreement's term, you will be liable to pay for any damage. So make sure you have in writing exactly what 'excess wear and tear' really entails, or else you could face a huge bill for just a few scratches.

buying from dealerships

Still the first place most people consider when buying a car, but dealerships are fast losing business to upstarts such as internet traders and importers. The reason for this is simple: perceived reputation. Buyers still think they are going into battle when they face a car salesman – that they are going to be fleeced by a smooth operator. It is certainly true that you need to keep your wits about you, but you can play them at their own game too.

The advantage of dealerships is that they offer the best post-sales comfort blanket available. Their close link to the manufacturers (many operate under a franchise arrangement) means that getting a quality service is easy. Of course, you also know exactly where to come back to if you have a problem, so always go for established dealerships that have a long-standing, solid reputation.

Don't enter a dealership cold without knowing anything about the

the test drive

Whether you're buying privately or from a dealership, you will typically be expected to sit in the passenger seat for the first few miles to be talked through all the car's 'plus' points. Wait patiently for the sales spiel to end by taking the time to watch and listen for any unexpected reactions from the car to the driving, such as unusual noises.

You will probably find that you will be handed the keys only when you are on a nice quiet stretch of road. If you are with someone from a dealership, ignore this offer and say that you want to go out alone for half an hour or so. They should let you do this and it is only when alone that you will be able to concentrate on evaluating the car. A private buyer, of course, will not let you out of sight with their car alone, so ask them to sit in the back seat.

When establishing whether you like the feel of the car analyse the following factors:

* Do the seat, steering wheel, roof and legroom leave you comfortable behind the wheel?
* Is there enough storage space for your needs?
* Does the clutch feel heavy?
* Do the brakes react well and securely?
* Can you accelerate well when overtaking and go up hills adequately?
* Is the gear change smooth?
* Are there blind spots when turning at junctions?
* Can you park, reverse and U-turn the car easily?
* How does it 'feel' in heavy traffic and on motorways?
* Do you feel comfortable sitting in the back and passenger seats?

Finally, you want to make sure you are insured before you test-drive any car. It is unlikely that anyone will let you in their car without insurance, but be aware that in some circumstances you will be expected to pay for it, namely, when test-driving expensive prestige cars and privately-owned cars from the classifieds.

models available: they will eat you alive. Watch out for those expensive extras running up the total, the nitty-gritty of any finance deals, and letting slip your exact budget too early. Impress on them that you are likely to be a loyal customer who, if you like their service, will come back time and again. Begin the haggling by knocking off at least 10 to 15 per cent off the list price, and ask for some of those meaningful extras to be thrown in. (Don't think you're winning if you secure free fluffy dice: you want something like a free sunroof or electric windows for your efforts.)

buying from the classified ads

In theory, buying a second-hand car from an ad in the press should be easy. Just circle the car you like the look of, give the owner a quick ring and away you go: no middleman to take a cut. But the truth is that you are putting your trust in someone from whom you have little chance of redress should the car turn out to be a wreck on its last breath.

When perusing the ads, only consider ads that are detailed, lack clichés and trade lingo such as 'one careful owner' and 'first to see will buy', and are not obviously placed by a trader (look out for numbers repeated elsewhere on the page and mobile numbers). Compare like-for-like prices for models and mileage in *Glass's Guide*, then ring a few you like the look of. If you arrange an inspection, make sure it is either at their home or workplace, and that everything you see is included in the price. Make sure they have the V5 registration document, service records and MOT to give you, and that you can go for a decent test drive.

When it gets to the price, always haggle. Remember that many people just want shot of the damn thing and will be keen for a quick sale, which is always to your advantage. Before finalizing any deal, though, get a reputable mechanic to give it a once-over for about £50 (can you really tell if it's a cut-and-shut?), run an HPI (Hire Purchase Information) check (**www.hpicheck.com**) to see whether the vehicle is legit, and finally make sure you can transfer any warranties over to your name. A full HPI check will cost about £35 per vehicle (the AA also performs a similar service from its website), so only run these checks when you are really sure this is the one for you.

Quick tip: When perusing the records of former owners, look out for PO Box addresses, as this is a clue that the car could be ex-rental, in other words, a car that has been driven hard and fast with little care.

buying from car supermarkets

Bargain hunters love the concept of the pile 'em high car super-markets. There's no pushy sales person to negotiate with and the price is basically fixed – low. You won't get a nice cup of coffee and a warm office to talk business (more like a windswept parking lot), but who cares if you are going to save literally thousands of pounds on most new models? Most car supermarkets sell imported cars or ex-fleet vehicles, which is good for saving money, but you must be extra-vigilant when checking that all the components are there as listed. Look out for transit scratches, missing spare ignition keys or a missing manufacturer's handbook. You also want to make sure the car meets UK specifications, and if new, has at least a year's manufacturer warranty. Visit their websites beforehand, though, to go through the prices and models currently available.

buying imports

Importing your car from abroad has been big news over the last few years, but it remains a potentially taxing method. Doing it yourself isn't recommended unless you're completely confident that you can negotiate (often in another language), that you will get the right UK specification, and that you have the time and energy to do it. The 25 per cent plus savings are enticing, but many people are sensible and leave it to a specialist agent. They will deal with the additional headaches of customs, VAT, registration, delivery etc. that can be a minefield for most of us. An agent will typically charge between £300 and £1,000 depending on the car and the level of service, but get everything in writing and pay your deposit on a credit card. Remember, though, that you will get a shorter manufacturer's warranty (one year rather than three, typically) by importing. For detailed advice, visit **www.carimporting.co.uk**.

Warning: Don't confuse importing from Europe (parallel imports) with importing from Japan (grey imports). Grey imports are second-hand cars (virtually unheard of in Japan) that are shipped over to the UK. The potential pitfalls are too long to list here and the whole process is rarely worth the hassle.

buying at auction

Another route that is best left to the professionals, but if you are brave enough to mix it with the pros and think you know your cars, then it can certainly be rewarding.

Go along to one first as an onlooker to get the hang of how it's done. Once you have familiarized yourself with the unique lingo – the 'golden hour', the 'ticket', 'all good' – spend some time examining the cars, as they will be sold 'as seen' and you won't have a chance to check them out with a mechanic. This also means that some of your normal consumer rights will not apply, so make sure you really know your stuff (or take a friend who does). Examine the auctioneer's terms and conditions extra carefully and set yourself a strict bidding limit.

To find a reputable local auctioneer, and for further advice, contact the Retail Motor Industry Federation on 0845 758 5350.

buying from the web

The internet is near invaluable nowadays for doing your research, but it can also be a great place to actually make your purchase, too. The lack of overheads means some great prices, but as with any online purchase, extra care needs to be taken to make sure you are dealing with a trustworthy, big-name firm. Begin by getting every-thing in writing from them, establish the source of your car (Europe or UK?) and make sure you still test-drive the model somewhere locally beforehand (just don't tell the dealer what you're up to).

PRIMARY RESOURCES

MOTORING ASSOCIATIONS

AA
tel: 0870 600 0371
www.theaa.com

RAC
tel: 0870 5722 722
www.rac.co.uk

TRADE SHOWS

British International Motor Show
(held in October at the NEC,
Birmingham)
tel: 0800 378985
www.motorshow.co.uk

ONLINE CLASSIFIEDS

www.autoseek.co.uk
www.autotrader.co.uk
www.carseller.co.uk
www.exchangeandmart.co.uk
www.fish4cars.co.uk
www.virtual-showroom.co.uk

CAR SUPERMARKET LISTINGS

www.car-supermarkets.com

ADDITIONAL ADVICE AND RESEARCH SOURCES

DVLA
tel: 0870 240 0009
www.dvla.gov.uk/welcome.htm

Honest John
www.honestjohn.co.uk

The Office of Fair Trading's advice
on buying cars
www.oft.gov.uk/Consumer/Your+
Rights+When+Shopping/
cars.html

Retail Motor Industry Federation
tel: 0845 758 5350
www.rmif.co.uk

UK vehicle taxation rates
www.dvla.gov.uk/vehicles/
taxation.htm

Vehicle Certification Agency's fuel-
consumption data
www.vcacarfueldata.org.uk

MAGAZINES

Auto Express
tel: 01454 642503
www.autoexpress.co.uk

Autotrader
tel: 0845 345 3450
www.autotrader.co.uk

Exchange & Mart
tel: 01202 445000
www.exchangeandmart.co.uk

Glass's price guides
tel: 01932 823823
www.glass.co.uk

Loot
tel: 0870 704 0000,
http://motors.loot.com

Parkers
tel: 0905 123 0123
www.parkers.co.uk
(NB: calls to the car-buying advice
hotline cost £1 a minute)

Top Gear
tel: 01795 414726
www.topgear.com

ONLINE RETAILERS AND IMPORTERS

www.autobytel.co.uk
www.autoeurop.co.uk
www.carseekers.co.uk
www.eurekar.com
www.jamjar.com
www.oneswoop.com
www.trade-sales.co.uk
www.virgincars.com

MANUFACTURERS

Alfa Romeo
tel: 0800 718000
www.alfaromeo.co.uk

Aston Martin
tel: 01908 610620
www.astonmartin.com

Audi
tel: 0800 699888
www.audi.co.uk

Bentley
tel: 01270 653653
www.rolls-royceandbentley.co.uk

BMW (Mini)
tel: 0800 325600
www.bmw.co.uk
www.mini.co.uk

Bristol Cars
tel: 020 7603 5554
www.bristolcars.co.uk

Chevrolet
tel: 020 8208 0022
www.chevroleteurope.com

Chrysler/Jeep
tel: 0800 616159
www.chryslerjeep.co.uk

Citroën
tel: 0870 606 9000
www.citroen.co.uk

Daewoo
tel: 0800 060606
www.daewoo-cars.co.uk

Daihatsu
tel: 0121 520 5000
www.daihatsu.co.uk

Ferrari
tel: 01784 436222
www.ferrari.co.uk

Fiat
tel: 0800 717000
www.fiat.co.uk

Ford
tel: 08457 111888
www.ford.co.uk
www.forddirectonline.co.uk

Honda
tel: 0845 200 8000
www.honda.co.uk

Hyundai
tel: 01494 428600
www.hyundai-car.co.uk

Jaguar
tel: 0800 708060
www.jaguar.com

Land Rover
tel: 0800 110110
www.landrover.co.uk

Lexus
tel: 0845 278 8888
www.lexus.co.uk

Mazda
tel: 0845 601 3147
www.mazda.co.uk

Mercedes-Benz
tel: 0800 1777 7777
www.mercedes-benz.co.uk

MG Rover
tel: 08457 186186
www.mg-rover.com

Mitsubishi
tel: 01285 655 777
www.mitsubishi-cars.co.uk

Morgan Motors
tel: 01684 573104
www.morgan-motor.co.uk

Nissan
tel: 01923 899334
www.nissan.co.uk

Perodua
tel: 020 8961 1255
www.perodua-uk.com

Peugeot
tel: 0845 200 1234
www.peugeot.co.uk

Porsche
tel: 08457 911911
www.porsche.co.uk

Proton
tel: 08000 521521
www.proton.co.uk

Renault
tel: 0800 525150
www.renault.co.uk

Rolls Royce
tel: 01270 255155
www.rollsroycemotorcars.co.uk

Rover
tel: 0800 620820
www.rover.co.uk

Saab
tel: 0800 626556
www.saab.co.uk

Seat
tel: 0500 222222
www.seat.co.uk

Skoda
tel: 0845 774 5745
www.skoda.co.uk

Subaru
tel: 0121 557 2112
www.subaru.co.uk

Suzuki
tel: 01892 707007
www.suzuki.co.uk

Toyota
tel: 0845 275 5555
www.toyota.co.uk

Vauxhall
tel: 0845 600 1500
www.vauxhall.co.uk

Volvo
tel: 08457 564636
www.volvocars.co.uk

VW
tel: 0800 711811
www.volkswagen.co.uk

computers

the basics

It's so difficult keeping up with the pace of computer technology these days that the geeks have even coined a name for it – Grove's Law. It's named after Andy Grove, the CEO of the dominant microchip manufacturer Intel, and is used to describe how computer components, such as Intel chips, are deemed virtually obsolete after just a year or so of use. Throw in the fact that computer prices fluctuate more wildly than a dotcom share price, and the consumer can soon feel intimidated by the sight of a computer shop.

So how are you expected to buy a computer without it (and you) becoming a laughing stock within a few months? The best response is just to give up worrying and concentrate instead on getting a machine that is tailored to your needs. Thus, the first question to answer is what do you need a computer for?

Are you after a machine that will let you type the odd letter, keep tabs on your monthly outgoings and occasionally log on to a website? Or do you want a powerful multimedia machine that will let you play the latest games, record music and create complex computer images?

The typical response is something in-between – a computer that will suit the needs of any family member. Therefore, to find a happy medium, whether you plan on buying a laptop or desktop, you should concentrate on making sure that you buy adequate memory, a fast-enough processor and a big-enough hard drive. These should be your principal concerns, but as recommended specifications change so frequently – at present, look for at least a 1 GHz processor, 128 MB of RAM (memory) and a 20 GB hard drive – you should begin by establishing what's on the market and for what price by flicking through some computer magazines and browsing online retailers. You will soon establish which features – DVD-ROM, modem, graphics card etc – come as standard.

When you are doing your research you will also soon realize that your first major decision is whether you want an Apple Macintosh (Mac) or a PC. Both systems have their detractors and loyal fans (more so Mac users), but for the average home user, the PC is still probably the more realistic option. Even though Macs look great and have a more intuitive interface, they tend to be about 30 per cent more expensive than an equivalently equipped PC and offer less in the way of software compatibility, especially games. What's more, the internet tends to be a slightly friendlier place for PC users, and now that Microsoft has finally delivered a stable operating system, Windows XP, PCs have (almost) lost their irritating reputation for crashing more than Macs.

desktop or laptop?

Once you have grappled with the Mac vs PC debate, your next task is to decide whether you want a laptop (notebook) or desktop. The old maxim was that desktops were for offices and homes, while laptops were for executives wanting to play solitaire on the red-eye from New York. Now the market is flooded with laptops that are hailed as genuine desktop alternatives – fantastic for those of us who don't have the luxury of a spare room to place a cumbersome and ugly beige tower.

But even though laptops are now packing an equal punch in terms of computer power, the desktop isn't defeated – yet. Desktops are still much cheaper than a like-for-like laptop, and, just as important, are easier to upgrade. There's no worrying about batteries running down, the bigger monitor actually lets you see what you are doing, and there's no fiddling around with a laptop's infuriating mouse pads. Laptops also tend to get very hot (all those tightly packed electrical components are only cooled by a little fan), and you can't automatically include laptops on your household insurance, unlike desktops. Laptops do deliver, though, when it comes to convenience, space consumption and, well…looks. (Can you really imagine Carrie in *Sex in the City* using a desktop to write her column?)

So if you really think that you are going to be out and about requiring instant access to a computer at any given moment, then get a laptop – or a good handheld computer, which is now at least half the price of a desktop. If you also suffer from an acute lack of space at home, a laptop may be the answer. But for most people, a desktop is still the practical option as well as best value for money.

When it comes to recommending the best manufacturers, impartial advice from retailers is hard to come by, but when the Consumer Association last assessed the leading brands (November 2001), it concluded, after a wide range of member surveys, that the 'most recommended' included – in no particular order – Dan, Apple, Dell, IBM, Evesham, Viglen and Sony. It added that popular direct sellers such as Time and Tiny seemed to regularly fail to score highly in its member surveys.

before you buy

So, you've seen a machine that you like the look of. You've wiggled the mouse around a bit, found the right specifications and let the sales staff show you around the machine. Now you need to start getting some price quotes – at least three. It is important that you make sure the quotes are for precisely the same manufacturer and model if you want to establish an exact price comparison between retailers (always double-check against some price-comparison websites – see 'primary resources'), but if, as is most likely, you are comparing different manufacturers, examine the whole package on offer.

Retailers seem to rejoice in enticing us with as many 'freebies' as possible – a 'generous' software bundle worth hundreds of pounds, the 'free' printer, scanner or digital camera – but don't get distracted. You still want the engine of the computer (memory, processor speed and hard-drive size) to be your principal concern. This is what you should really be comparing.

Do you really think that printer (which will be of questionable quality in most cases) is 'free'? Do you really need that garden-design software or dinosaur encyclopedia? (It will only clog up your hard drive anyway.) Watch out for headline prices in adverts. They invariably fail to include VAT and delivery charges, and are often accompanied by a slew of jargon.

It is rarely worth opting for the state-of-the-art, cutting-edge machine, either. It will be disproportionately expensive and is more liable to develop teething problems. Look for machines that the computer magazines have broadly recommended and that have been on the market for least a few months. Remember, though, that magazines can sometimes slate a machine for being 0.01 of a second slower than a rival – a matter of concern for only true geeks – so read their reviews carefully and with your needs in mind.

Once you have settled on a computer you like the look of, the next task is to quiz the retailer (and the manufacturer in some cases) about their terms of sale. Ensure that you ask them all of these following questions and have every one satisfactorily answered:

* Do I have everything I need to get the product up and running when I get it home?
* What is the total price of getting the computer to my home?
* How can I pay? (Do you have a better rate for cash? Or an interest-free payment scheme? What are your financing terms and rates?)
* How long will delivery take?
* Is the product in stock today?
* What precisely is your returns policy?
* Do you have a technical help support line? (How are calls charged? Does it offer 24-hour support?)
* Do you have support personnel in my area?
* If the computer requires repairing, do I have to pay for it to be returned to the shop, or will a technician come to me (known respectively as return-to-base and onsite repairs)?

The question of warranties demands special attention. Most retailers will offer some kind of extended warranty to you, typically for an annual fee. What you need to ask yourself is whether it is really worth the cost. Only two to three warranties out of ten sold are ever used by customers, and the retailers are usually making a hefty profit on them. You are usually better off employing a local computer repair specialist to come and sort out your problem. Don't forget either that most manufacturers include a one-year guarantee as standard with machines.

Even if you don't intend buying an extended warranty, it is often worth quizzing the retailer about them anyway, as they are a good indicator of their quality of service. If they push them without explanation of the terms, should you really trust them to provide you with an unbiased view on the machine itself?

buying from the high street

Even though you will get much better advice from a local small-scale computer specialist, sadly, you are still likely to get the best deals from the big nationwide stores such as PC World and Tiny. In addition, while the nationwide electrical goods retailers on the high street – such as Dixons, Currys and Comet – offer much less choice, they have the advantage of being strong, well-known retail brands, which is still an important factor for the first-time computer shopper.

Where the giant retailers fail, though, is in their lack of adequate choice, lack of true expertise among sales staff and expensive, often-criticized extended warranty schemes. The best advice is to use the big computer retailers for your research purposes, but to use a trusted internet site or mail-order retailer to actually make your purchase.

The exception to the rule, however, is London's Tottenham Court Road, which is known as the country's electrical goods epicentre. The area has a reputation as a bazaar peopled with fast-talking, quick-witted pros who let the colour of your money do the talking, and who are not familiar with the concept of the fixed price. In reality, it does offer great value, particularly for laptops, but, as ever, shop around, do plenty of research, talk finance and bounce quotes off rival stores. Cash does talk, but you are more likely to get good deals buying a few products at once and asking for their 'best price'.

software: a quick tip

Quality software – such as the ever-popular Microsoft Office – is rarely included in the price of computers. Before spending hundreds of pounds on expensive software, consider Microsoft's Student Licence scheme. If you are a student, a parent with children in education or a teacher, you can register for savings of up to 80 per cent. MS Office XP Standard is usually £400 or so: with the Student Licence deal, it will cost about £100. For more information, telephone 0870 607 0800 or visit www.microsoft.com/uk/education/studentlicence.

only for the brave

If you think you know your SD-RAM memory from your DDR memory, then you could consider buying from a computer fair (see 'primary resources'), where machines and components can be picked up at rock-bottom prices. They're certainly not for the nervy novice though.

buying online

If value for money is what you crave, then buying online is, without doubt, your best option. As long as you follow a few golden rules, buying a computer online is safe, convenient and cheaper than via any high-street retailer.

Begin by comparing prices. This can mean consulting any website in the world, but for tax and delivery reasons you are best sticking to sites based in the UK, Europe and the US.

When you know which model you want to buy, type it into a search engine to get information such as reviews and into a price-comparison site to get a broad range of quotes. When you have a shortlist of about three, visit the sites in question and find the following information:

* Does it provide a secure shopping environment? (Look for the little padlock symbol in the bottom left-hand corner of the browser.)
* Does it offer the same terms of delivery, quality, warranties and so on that a bricks-and-mortar retailer is prepared to offer?
* Does the deal sound too good to be true when compared against other equivalent offerings? If so, it probably is.

You will soon discover that foreign sites usually offer better deals than the UK ones, but you have to remember the extra costs of importing something like a computer. If you buy from a UK site, you don't have to worry about currency conversions. In addition, the VAT will be added at source, and delivery will be easier to organize.

If you buy from an EU-based site, you don't have to pay Customs and Excise duty, but you will have to pay whatever the local VAT rate is. Germany's rate, for example, is 16 per cent compared to the UK's

ethics watch

When *Ethical Consumer* magazine looked at the computer industry in June 2000, it expressed concern about the number of obsolete computers entering the waste stream. Levels of waste electrical equipment in the UK are increasing at six times the rate of other domestic and industrial waste, and computers make up almost half of the total. The report also detailed how most of the major PC manufacturers had been involved in lobbying against EU environmental legislation designed to deal with the problem.

In addition, over half of the top twenty UK brands were involved in the arms trade, and none of the major manufacturers operated a code of conduct for working conditions at supplier companies. Three European eco-labelling schemes exist for computer equipment, the most stringent of which is the Swedish TCO scheme (TCO95 or TCO99 were especially recommended).

Ethical Consumer's best buys were Dan, Dell, Sun Microsystems, Time and Tiny – although, of course, a key recommendation was to look at second-hand options first. For more information, visit www.ethicalconsumer.org or call 0161 226 2929.

17.5 per cent. (VAT-registered businesses will be able to avoid paying VAT if they buy within the EU.)

Things get a bit more complicated when buying from a website that is based outside the EU. Local taxation will vary greatly (in the US taxes vary from state to state), and delivery costs will be much higher. The real sting in the tail is that Customs and Excise will now want a slice of the action, too. Goods that cost less than £18 (£36 if they're a gift) are exempt, but anything over that will be liable for duty and VAT.

Luckily, IT hardware is currently exempt from duty charges, thus saving you the 3.5 per cent extra that you would have to pay for something like a CD, but VAT will still apply. When the goods arrive, the delivery company or Post Office will expect you to pay the VAT (and a processing fee of up to about £5) on delivery, so make sure you have worked out all the costs. For extra information, ring HM Custom and Excise's National Advice Service on 0845 010 9000. Try to buy your computer with a credit card for added protection, particularly if buying from a UK-based site.

Don't forget that some manufacturers offer computers that have been returned for whatever reasons by customers at a much-reduced price. More often than not, the computers haven't even been used (by bankrupt firms, for example), but they cannot be sold as new for legal reasons. Manufactures such as Dell Outlet refurbish and fully retest the machines and all the normal guarantees apply. Contact Dell Outlet on 0870 905 0150 or visit www.euro.dell.com/countries/uk/enu/dfo for details.

Other popular manufacturers that offer similar schemes are IBM (go to www.ibm.com/uk and type in 'buy refurbished equipment online' into the site's search facility), and Compaq (www.compaqworks.com is Compaq's US-based outlet shop so be aware that the warranties may not be valid if bought for a UK delivery).

expert view

Tips for buying a home PC by Paul Sanders, editor of *Computer Buyer* magazine:

* To get the right PC, you need to consider what you'll use it for. List on paper what you'll be doing and tell every salesperson you talk to – then if they sell you something inappropriate, you'll qualify for a refund under the Sales of Goods Act. Basic desktop internet PCs shouldn't cost more than £600; games PCs need more power, and start from £800.

* Even if you become an expert on PCs, there are some things you simply can't tell from specifications. For instance, the monitor and the system speed call for hands-on laboratory testing. Consult the reviews in computer magazines for definitive verdicts.

* Portability adds a new dimension to computing – but you pay for it in many ways. Besides being more expensive, laptops have fewer features, are never as fast as desktop PCs, and are generally useless for games. If you're buying your first PC, you should definitely go for a desktop.

* Remember to ask about battery life when buying a laptop, and halve it for a more realistic estimate. Notebooks are particularly worth trying before you buy, paying particular attention to the keyboard, 'mouse' pointer, screen and general sturdiness. London's Tottenham Court Road is a great place to browse, bargain and buy.

* Big PC cases may be an eyesore, but small ones may use lower-quality 'integrated' components and will certainly be harder to upgrade.

* Printers, scanners and cameras 'thrown in' with PC systems are often of the very lowest quality. If you were planning to buy Microsoft Office, however, a bundled version will do just as well, lacking just the flimsy manual and telephone support that accompany the full retail version.

* Watch out for 'five-year warranties' that switch from covering parts and labour to just labour after a year or two. On-site warranties sound great, but are often overpriced and may be more hassle than simply sending your PC back for repair. Don't pay for extended warranties, save up instead – most people replace their PC every five years.

PRIMARY RESOURCES

MAGAZINES

Computer Buyer
tel: 01454 642503
www.computerbuyer.co.uk

Computer Shopper
tel: 01454 642503
www.compshopper.co.uk

Maximum PC
tel: 01458 271152
www.maximumpc.co.uk

PC Format
tel: 020 7903 6800
www.pcformat.co.uk

PC Magazine
tel: 020 7903 6800
www.pcmag.co.uk

PC Plus
tel: 020 7903 6800
www.pcplus.co.uk

PC Pro
tel: 01454 642503
www.pcpro.co.uk

Personal Computer World
tel: 020 7316 9862
www.pcw.co.uk

What PC?
tel: 020 7316 9862
www.whatpc.co.uk

TECHNICAL REFERENCE SITE

www.pctechguide.com

MANUFACTURERS

Acer
tel: 0870 900 2237
www.acer.co.uk

Advent
Available from PC World, Dixons
and Currys

AJP
tel: 020 8208 9755
www.ajp.co.uk

Apple
tel: 0800 783 4846
www.apple.com

Armari
tel: 020 8993 4111
www.armari.com

Axon
tel: 01279 306868
www.axon.ltd.uk

Compaq
tel: 0845 270 4000
www.compaq.co.uk

Dan
tel: 0870 444 7010
www.dan.co.uk

Dell
tel: 0870 907 4000
www.dell.co.uk

Elonex
tel: 0800 037 4462
www.elonex.co.uk

Evesham
tel: 0800 038 0800
www.evesham.com

Fujitsu-Siemens
tel: 0808 100 2225
www.fujitsu-siemens.com

hp (formerly Hewlett Packard)
tel: 08705 474747
www.hp.com/uk

Hi-Grade Computers
tel: 0800 074 0403
www.higrade.com

IBM
tel: 0800 169 1461
www.ibm.com/uk/

Mesh
tel: 020 8208 4744
www.meshcomputers.com

Packard Bell
tel: 01628 512400
www.packardbell.co.uk

Panrix
tel: 0113 2444 958
www.panrix.com

Sony
tel: 08705 424424
www.sony.co.uk

Time
tel: 0800 771107
www.timecomputers.com

Tiny
tel: 0800 821333
www.tiny.com

Toshiba
tel: 01932 828828
www.toshiba.co.uk

Viglen
tel: 020 8758 7000
www.viglen.co.uk

ONLINE RETAILERS

Action
 tel: 0800 333333
 www.action.com

Buy.com
 tel: 0800 376 5959
 www.buy.com

Currys
 tel: 0500 304304
 www.currys.co.uk

Dabs Direct
 tel: 0800 674467
 www.dabs.com

Dixons
 tel: 08000 682868
 www.dixons.co.uk

Javelin
 tel: 01254 505505
 www.javelincomputers.com

Jigsaw24
 tel: 0115 916 5599
 www.jigsaw24.com

John Lewis
 tel: 08456 049049
 www.johnlewis.com

Jungle.com
 tel: 0800 0355 3555
 www.jungle.com

Lapland
 tel: 01256 867700
 www.lapland.co.uk

Lowcost Computers
 tel: 01258 817437
 www.lowcost-computers.co.uk

Mac Warehouse
 tel: 08705 168740
 www.macwarehouse.co.uk

Micro Anvika
 tel: 020 7467 6050
 www.microanvika.co.uk

Microwarehouse
 tel: 08705 168671
 www.microwarehouse.co.uk

PC World
 tel: 08000 565732
 www.pcworld.co.uk

Simply Computers
 tel: 0800 035 2100
 www.simply.co.uk

Watford Electronics
 tel: 0870 729 5600
 www.watford.co.uk

COMPUTER FAIRS

www.afm96.co.uk
www.computer-fairs.co.uk

PRICE-COMPARISON WEBSITES

www.checkaprice.com
www.computerprices.co.uk
www.dealtime.co.uk
www.easyvalue.com
www.mysimon.com
www.pcindex.co.uk
www.2020shops.com
http://uk.kelkoo.com
http://uk.shopping.yahoo.com/
 computers
http://uk.shopsmart.com

designer clothes

the basics

'Fashion is something that goes in one year and out the other.' It's an old joke, but it helps to explain why many of us get the jitters when we need to buy something smart, fashionable, or preferably both. These are the special occasions when we need to look our absolute best – interviews, weddings, dates, meeting the in-laws – and when most of us are immediately struck down with the common affliction known as IWD, or Instant Wardrobe Dismissal (the principal telltale symptom being when you start screaming 'I don't have anything to wear' while standing before your dressing mirror).

The most common remedy is to grab your flexible friend (and your credit card), and head for the shops. Hours later, you're home, your feet are killing you, your blood pressure is 180/105, your bank manager's pressure is soon to be even higher, but, by God, you've found something you're going to love wearing. Surely there has to be another way – and one that doesn't involve calling in *What Not To Wear*'s Susannah and Trinny.

Assuming that you, or better still, your best friend is capable of knowing what you look best in, your principal concern is finding something that isn't going to break the bank and is also a pleasure to buy. And while most of us are suckers for designer labels and the often-questionable kudos associated with wearing them, they need not cost the big sums found on those small price tags. Thankfully, the designer shopper now has many options that don't include those intimidating and super-pricey Bond Street boutiques.

buying from the high street

Everyone knows that the best time to hit the high street is when the sales are on. The two big sales periods are typically from Boxing Day to early January and then early July. Many retailers will knock up to 50 per cent, possibly more, off designer labels, but many sale items are last season's stock, which in high-fashion terms is like investing in pebble-dashing for your home. The only true sales prize is the reduced classic item, one that could be worn by itself or as a separate in years to come. Unsurprisingly, finding one of these in the bun fight that is a sale is tricky.

There has been a move over the last few years for some supermarkets to import cheaper 'grey-market' designer goods from abroad, and pass on the savings to their consumer. Sadly, in November 2001, Tesco lost its claim to import Levi's 501 jeans from cheaper wholesalers abroad, because it was not selling them in the 'correct environment' expected by the design houses. It was a blow to the grey-market importers, but keep an eye out for future attempts.

Shopping on the high street doesn't have to be restricted to this country, however. Day-trippers across the Channel speak of competitive prices. The traditional destinations of Calais and Dieppe may not offer, let's say, the cutting-edge labels you may be after, but many shoppers speak highly of the range on offer among the shops in the Belgian port of Ostend.

It may not be what you were really thinking of, but don't ignore charity shops either. Vintage clothing is all the rage, and you never know what you may find. There are also many shops – as well as the popular markets found at, for example, Portobello, Camden and Greenwich in London – that now specialize in selling vintage designer labels (see 'primary resources').

What you must be careful of, though, is counterfeit designer goods. Holidaymakers to the Far East are all too aware of such goods, but they are increasingly making their way to the UK high street. Poor imitations can often be seen being flogged by dodgy geezers on busy high streets such as London's Oxford Street, outside busy stations and at markets. While some people knowingly buy such goods, and may even boast about them (some fake items from

New York's Canal Street are seen in such a light), remember that the quality will invariably be dire and that you are party to an illegal act.

buying from designer sales

All true shopaholics and fashionistas know about designer sales. These aren't the high-street sales beloved by the masses, but rather small-scale affairs in which you often have to be on a mailing list or a paid-up member to be invited (see 'primary resources'). Some will be sample sales of particular designers, some may offer shop returns, some may be put on by wholesalers, but whatever is being offered, you will find savings of up to 90 per cent on retail prices. You won't get a large selection of sizes and may not have the luxury of a changing room, but for that kind of savings, who cares? Unfortunately, most are them are located in London.

One accessible designer sale to look out for in particular is London Fashion Weekend, which, yes, follows London Fashion Week in February. Over one hundred leading designers sell their wares at reduced prices, and tickets cost £8.50.

buying from factory outlets

The nineties saw the rise of the out-of-town shopping village in the UK. These family- (and car-) friendly clusters of shops are different from the shopping malls typified by Kent's Bluewater or Gateshead's MetroCentre, in that they are often the exclusive home of factory outlets – no-frills shops selling designer goods at wholesale prices.

There are more than twenty such villages located around the country, offering all manner of wholesale goods (see 'primary resources'), but some have a particular bent towards designer clothes. The one offering possibly the highest-quality clothes is Oxfordshire's Bicester Village, where names such as Versace and Paul Smith can be found, but many other villages offer designer labels.

Like designer sales, many of the items on sale are end-of-range, cancelled orders, returns, odd sizes or last season's stock. But you need to be aware of a few facts before speeding off to the nearest village. Prices aren't guaranteed to be lower than those found on the high street and, perhaps more importantly, not all the clothes for sale were ever intended to make it to the high street. Do you really think a manufacturer could stay in business if it mismanaged its stock so badly that it could keep a factory outlet in permanent business? For this reason, make sure you know what is available, and for what price, on the high street first. Also consider these other tips when outlet shopping:

- Try to visit outlets on weekdays, preferably in the morning. About 80 per cent of shoppers show up at the weekend.

- Look for off-season bargains, such as swimsuits in the autumn and winter coats and skiing clobber in late spring.

- Quality can vary wildly, so always check the zips, buttons and stitching carefully.

- Most outlets tend to be best for items like designer shirts, jeans, children's clothes and sportswear, rather than items like a little black cocktail dress or morning suit.

- Note that many outlets reduce prices even further when the high-street retailers hold their big sales.

- It is wise to ring ahead of any visit to find out exactly which names and types of clothing an outlet stocks to save any wasted visits.

- Be careful when buying 'seconds'. If a defect is pointed out to you before you buy, you will lose your right of return.

buying from the web

As ever, the internet offers the bargain hunter plenty of value. Many sites have now sprung up offering discounted designer clothes (some even have sales), and if you know what you are after and are confident that you don't need to try on a particular size first, you should always add a quick trawl of the web to your regular ground-work. Of course, the cost of shipping is a large consideration when buying online, and don't forget that if you need to return any item, for whatever reason, you will have to pay for the return shipping costs.

For convenience and peace of mind, it's probably best to stick to the well-known sites that are based in the UK (see 'primary resources'), but if you do find something on a foreign site, work out how much tax and excise you will need to pay – it might make you change your mind.

If it's vintage clothes you're after, a few sites – mainly based in the US – specialize in this area, but it might also be worth having a quick look on the online auctions such as those found at **www.ebay.co.uk**.

buying bespoke clothing

Having a tailor-made suit is a rarity these days, but it need not be. While a tailor on London's Savile Row will expect you to part with between £500 and £3,000 for one suit, dapper chaps (and dames) do have alternative ways in which to have a suit made to fit.

Many of us find the prospect – and the cost – of having a team of tailors busying themselves around our inside leg a little daunting (yes, if you're a man, they may well ask you which 'side' you dress), but the comfort and appearance of a tailored suit cannot be matched by any ready-to-wear designer label offering.

Before you start ringing round local tailors, though, you must be settled on the style and type of cloth you would like. Flick through as many fashion magazines as you can, ripping out all the styles you like so that you can take them with you to show the tailor. To get an idea of the type of cloth you may like, you can buy samples for 50p from **www.fabricsite.co.uk**. Although pure wool is the preferred choice of most bespoke tailors, you should consider that a quality 80/20 blend of wool and synthetic material will wear just as well as a suit made of 100 per cent wool, and the difference in the 'hand', or feel, of the cloth will be near-indistinguishable. What's more, it will be about 20 per cent cheaper.

A much cheaper alternative than the local tailor, however, is to get your suit made by a visiting tailor from the Far East. For years, people have been returning from trips to Hong Kong, Singapore and India with bespoke suits made for a fraction of the price they would have paid back home. Now some of those tailors are travelling the world to come to their customers (see 'primary resources').

Perhaps the best-known of these travelling tailors is Raja Fashions from Hong Kong. Representatives tour the hotel suites of the world's leading cities measuring up visiting clients. They then email the measurements to their colleagues back in Hong Kong along with a photograph of the client. The suit is then made and posted to the client in under four weeks. Not bad for a bespoke suit that will cost you around £100.

You also have the choice of getting a package of tailored items that could include, for example, blazers, extra trousers, extra skirts, or coats. Many people swear by such services, but one criticism is that visiting tailors need to be controlled and guided with precision when it comes to keeping in touch with current fashions. If you like your look to be this side of the Bay City Rollers, then direct the tailors as much as possible. Ask to see examples of suits they have already made and take a friend along to help keep the situation under control.

A good tip to remember when having a suit made by any tailor is to get two pairs of trousers made for each suit. Trousers always show the first signs of wear and tear, and if you can be organized enough to alternate the two pairs, you should be able to extend the life of the suit.

ethics watch

When *Ethical Consumer* magazine last looked at the clothing industry, the main issue highlighted was the use of sweatshop labour in the Far East and Eastern Europe. UK companies commonly subcontract orders overseas, where hours are long, pay low and conditions poor. More information is available on this subject at www.labourbehindthelabel.org.

With conventional cotton cultivation using large amounts of water and pesticides, readers concerned about environmental issues were advised to look for organic cotton clothing.

Taking into account social, environmental and animal welfare issues, *Ethical Consumer*'s Best Buy recommendations were a range of small independent clothing chains, which are listed at www.ethicalconsumer.org/magazine/clothing_buyers_guide_directory.htm.

For a low-cost alternative, the magazine advised second-hand clothing from charity shops and vintage outlets.

The mainstream best buys were companies involved in the government-backed Ethical Trading Initiative on improving labour standards overseas. They may not all be designer labels, but they currently include Levi's, Littlewoods, M&S, Mothercare and Monsoon.

For more information, visit www.ethicalconsumer.org or call 0161 226 2929.

expert view

Womenswear buying tips from the fashion team at *Drapers Record*, the weekly trade magazine for the fashion business (tel: 01858 438847, **www.drapersrecord.com**).

* Know what colours suit you by holding the garment to your face and seeing the effect on your skin tone. But remember that shop lights can distort the colours. You definitely can wear something other than black, but think carefully about colour combinations.

* Know your size – and don't kid yourself. You will not slim down to fit into something. Don't be fooled by what it says on the label – there is no consistency in sizing between fashion companies or fashion chains, so try it on first.

* Always take the right shoes and the right underwear with you when you are shopping. For example, take your evening shoes, not your trainers, when you are going to buy an evening outfit. Similarly, make sure you try something on with the appropriate bra and knickers.

* Only buy classics in the sale. Be very disciplined when faced with a 'bargain'. If you would not buy the item at full price, don't bother with it at a reduced price.

* Don't take your husband, boyfriend or lover with you when you go shopping. They will quickly become bored and distract you from your task. Rather, take a girlfriend. They will be more interested and will give you an honest opinion of how you look in that ridiculous outfit you are considering.

* Check the returns policy of the retailer. They are not obliged to give you your money back just because you have had second thoughts when you get home. And never take something back after wearing it because you fancy something else – it's dishonest.

* Don't dismiss something just because it doesn't have what's known in the trade as 'hanger appeal'. Something that looks dull on the hanger can look fabulous when tried on. So try it on.

* If you have to stop and really think about buying something, you probably don't need it and won't wear it very often if you do buy it.

* Try out the personal shopping service offered by the bigger department stores and chains. You will be guided by a sales consultant who can act as a well-informed friend.

* Calculate the price-per-wear ratio when you are looking at expensive clothes. If it costs £500, but you can wear it twice a week, it makes sense.

* Be aware of what you already have in your wardrobe. A new item in a new colour will also mean new shoes, accessories and pieces to complete the outfit.

Most fashion brands and fashion sales agents sell off their samples at the end of the selling season (about four months before the stuff actually hits the shops). If you are sample size (normally size 12), you can pick up the bargains for the wholesale price, plus VAT. Most are in the fashion district around Oxford Circus in central London, but there are plenty of fashion agents in, for example, Manchester, Leeds and Glasgow.

A key accessory is a good and sometimes inexpensive way to update your existing wardrobe.

Befriend a sales assistant at your local shop. Get her to tell you when new stuff is arriving. You will find this sort of service is more readily available at an independent shop, rather than a multiple. You may have to pay a bit more for your fashion, but you get a completely different service experience.

Take a good look at the care labels. Do you really want the cost of dry-clean-only garments? Manufacturers sometimes do protect themselves by recommending dry cleaning when careful washing will do, but once something is ruined, it stays ruined.

PRIMARY RESOURCES

ONLINE RETAILERS

www.affordabledesigners.co.uk
www.bbclothing.co.uk
www.brandedstocks.co.uk
www.buy-jeans.net
www.clothesdirect.co.uk
www.clothingtrends.co.uk
www.designerdiscount.co.uk
www.haburi.com
www.net-a-porter.com
www.styleshopdirect.com
www.ukdesignershop.com
www.yoox.com

DESIGNER SALES

100% Original (held in east London four times a year)
tel: 020 7923 0044

British Designer Sale (held at London's Chelsea Town Hall five times a year)
tel: 020 7228 5314
(membership costs £32 a year)

Designer Sales (held at London's Brick Lane five times a year)
tel: 01273 470880
www.designersales.co.uk
(£2 admission)

Designer Warehouse Sales (held near London's King's Cross station about ten times a year)
tel: 020 7704 1064
www.dwslondon.co.uk

Ghost warehouse sale (held annually at its warehouse on London's Kensal Road)
tel: 020 8960 3121
www.ghost.co.uk

London Fashion Weekend (held in February after London Fashion Week)
tel: 0870 735 2222
www.londonfashionweek.co.uk

Really Good Deal Fashion Sale
(held at Ascot Racecourse twice a
year)
  tel: 01367 860017
  (£5 admission)

Session Sales (held at London's
Chiswick Town Hall eight times a
year)
  tel: 020 8994 4983
  (membership costs £29.50 a year)

SHOPPING VILLAGES

Bicester Village, Oxfordshire
  tel: 01869 323200

Cheshire Oaks Designer Outlet,
The Wirral
  tel: 0151 348 5600

Clarks Village Factory Shopping,
Somerset
  tel: 01458 840064

Festival Park Factory Shopping
Village, Gwent
  tel: 01495 350010

Freeport Castleford Outlet Village,
West Yorkshire
  tel: 01977 520153
  www.freeportplc.com

Freeport Fleetwood Outlet Village,
Lancashire
  tel: 01253 877377
  www.freeportplc.com

Great Western Designer Outlet,
Wiltshire
  tel: 01793 507600

McArthurGlen Designer Outlet
Livingston, West Lothian
  tel: 01506 423600
  www.mcarthurglen.com

Royal Quays Outlet Centre, Tyne
and Wear
  tel: 0191 296 3743

For a full list, visit
www.shoppingvillages.com
or telephone 01746 780382

VINTAGE CLOTHING RETAILERS

Affleck's Palace (52 Church Street,
Manchester)
  tel: 0161 834 2039

Cornucopia (12 Upper Tachbrook
Street, London SW1)
  tel: 020 7828 5752

Real McCoy (21 The Fore Street
Centre, Fore Street, Exeter)
  tel: 01392 410481

Rellick (6 Golborne Road,
London W10)
  tel: 020 8962 0089

Steinberg & Tolkien (193 King's
Road, Chelsea, London)
  tel: 020 7376 3660

Also try:
  www.antiquedress.com
  www.carolinesclosets.com
  www.rustyzipper.com
  www.vintagecouture.com
  www.vintagevixen.com

TRAVELLING TAILORS

Ash Samtani Clothing Ltd
  tel: 00852 2367 4285
  www.samtani.com

Intercontinent Tailors
  tel: 00852 2367 8495
  www.intailors.com

Raja Fashions
  tel: 00852 2366 7624
  www.raja-fashions.com

LEADING DESIGNER LABELS

For an exhaustive list of the
leading designers and their
contact details, including
websites, visit:
www.fashionwindows.com/fashion
_designers/showall_fashion
_designers.asp

TRADE ASSOCIATIONS

Association of Suppliers to
Clothing Industry
  tel: 01422 354666
  www.asbci.co.uk

British Fashion Council
  tel: 020 7636 7788
  www.londonfashionweek.co.uk

British Menswear Guild
  tel: 020 7580 8783
  www.british-menswear-guild.co.uk

International Association of
Clothing Designers and Executives
  tel: 001 603 672 4065
  www.iacde.com

diamond rings

the basics

If you're planning on joining the 75 per cent of British men who buy their 'special lady' a diamond engagement ring, then you will want to pay very, very close attention to the following advice. This is certainly not something you want to get wrong. Not only are you about to part with a substantial amount of money (you must be warned that all women know the engagement ring mantra that the fiancé should be waving goodbye to at least a month's salary), but you are also about to purchase an object that will – hopefully – be a permanent symbol of your life's most important relationship. So then, the pressure is on.

The good news is that there are some universally agreed guidelines for buying diamonds. Follow them and you should avoid the pitfall of buying a tacky piece of cut glass that even Gerald Ratner – the man who said even a prawn sandwich would last longer than his jewellery – would be ashamed to offload. But let's get the geology lesson over with first, as you'll no doubt want to know why diamonds are valued so highly. It will also help you appreciate the guidelines a little better.

Diamonds are 99.95 per cent pure crystallized carbon and can be extremely old – one to three billion years old, in fact. They are the hardest naturally occurring substance known and are formed beneath the Earth's surface when ancient volcanoes erode down, releasing diamond crystals from their feed-pipes into layers of gravel that are later mined. However, due to the relative rarity of this natural process, mines are located in just a handful of sites around the world. In rough form, diamonds are then shipped to the world's few cutting centres to be shaped and polished before being set in jewellery. Admittedly, none of this sounds very romantic, but it's the hardness, brilliance and sparkle of diamonds that make them a girl's best friend.

Now for a quick history lesson, as you'll be curious to know where the custom began. (You might even impress her with this bit, too.) Legend dictates that in 1477, a love-struck Austrian by the name of Archduke Maximilian came up with a gem of an idea: why not give Mary of Burgundy a diamond ring to celebrate their imminent engagement? He placed it on the third finger of her left hand, the finger believed by ancient Egyptians to have a vein that led straight to the heart. It is not known whether the marriage was a success, but you don't need to get into that for your purposes.

the 4Cs

So now you know why you're buying an engagement ring made with a diamond, you can familiarize yourself with the famous '4Cs', namely cut, colour, clarity and carat. All must be considered equally when comparing diamonds, but more than any other factor, according to Tiffany and Co., it is how the diamond is cut that will determine its defining characteristic.

cut

As the only characteristic of a diamond that is not influenced by nature, the cut is open to mistakes and bad practices. Cut a diamond incorrectly and the defining sparkle will be compromised. It is how the fifty-seven or fifty-eight facets (the tiny planes cut on the diamond's surface) are angled and sized that dictates how light reflects and exits the diamond, an effect known as its 'fire'. Make the cuts too deep or too shallow and the diamond will be less brilliant.

The cut will also determine the shape of the diamond. The most common shape is the round cut, but other shapes include the emerald, the pear, the marquise, the princess, the oval and the heart-shaped cut. Ask to see all of these shapes, if only in a picture, to make sure you have covered all your options.

colour

The most valuable and rare colour is white, that's to say colourless. Jewellers grade absolutely colourless diamonds with a 'D'. The scale moves up to 'Z' – don't ask what happened to A, B and C – and in-between these two extremes, diamonds will display very subtle coloured tones. Diamonds with a very strong and distinct colour are also extremely rare and are called fancies.

clarity

Many people get unnecessarily hung up about the clarity of a diamond. Look into most diamonds with a jeweller's loupe (magnifying eyepiece) and you will see small 'inclusions', also known as 'nature's fingerprints'. They look like small clouds or feathers, but are usually invisible to the naked eye. Inclusions can affect the diamond's fire, but they also make your diamond unique and shouldn't always be seen as a fault. Why worry too much about something you can't see anyway? As long as the stone is graded SI1 (Slightly Included 1) or better (best and most expensive is IF, or Internally Flawless; worst is I3, or Imperfect 3), you should be OK.

carat

The weight and thus size of a diamond is measured according to its carat. A carat is equal to 0.2 gram, or 200 milligrams. A carat is divided into one hundred smaller units called 'points'. So, for example, three quarters of a carat is 75 points. The average size of most engagement ring diamonds is somewhere between one carat and half a carat. (Don't confuse diamond carats with the unit of purity for gold.)

Any jeweller worth their salt should know about the 4Cs and be willing to talk you through them all without being asked when displaying diamonds. But if you don't wish to place your entire trust in a jeweller, you should request a 'cert stone' – a diamond that has been assessed, graded and coded with a laser by an independent gemmological laboratory. The type of the certificate is important, as not all enjoy universal recognition. The most internationally recognized are issued by the GIA (Gemmological Institute of America). Other popular certificates include HRD, IGL, EGL and AGS (see 'primary resources'). The fee for a grading certificate varies according to the carat of your diamond, but for exact prices, contact a specific lab. And do not be afraid of organizing your own certificate, rather than simply opting for the jeweller's recommendation.

Another good reason for getting cert stones is to guard against buying 'diamonds' made with substitutes. Zircon, white sapphire, topaz and quartz are natural minerals that can be nearly colourless and therefore used as natural diamond substitutes. Synthetic substitutes include cubic zirconia and moissanite. All these are sold legitimately as cheap alternatives, but be aware that they are sometimes, albeit rarely, passed off as real diamonds.

Diamonds can also be artificially treated, most commonly by being fracture-filled, irradiated or laser-treated. All of this is legal, as long as it is disclosed to the buyer, but if you want a 'real' and untreated diamond guard yourself against terms like 'clarity enhanced'.

ethics watch: 'blood diamonds'

It is understandable to want to ask a jeweller about the origin of a diamond. After all, do you really want to be buying a diamond if your money is complicit in helping to arm a rogue government or militia group with a questionable human rights record? Unfortunately, the location of some of the world's key diamond mines happens to coincide with the location of some of the world's most bitter conflicts. Sierra Leone is perhaps the most infamous at present, but the diamond trade has been linked by the UN to troubles in other African states, including Rwanda, Angola, Liberia, the Central African Republic, Congo–Brazzaville, Uganda, Ghana, Namibia, Mali, Zambia, Burkina Faso, Guinea and the Ivory Coast.

The UN has also criticized Switzerland, not a diamond-producing nation but a diamond free-trade area, for its role as a transit point for almost half the rough diamonds entering Britain. Antwerp, the 'diamond capital of the world', is also criticized for 'facilitating' the trade in so-called 'blood diamonds'.

Sadly, as consumers, we are currently helpless when it comes to accurately establishing the true origin of a cut diamond. 'After the diamond is cut,' says Stephen Kennedy, the laboratory director at the Gemmological Association and Gem Testing Laboratory of Great Britain, 'there is no way of knowing where it came from.' His only advice is to be suspicious of dealers who suggest otherwise. The UN's advice is to exercise consumer power by always asking about the origin of diamonds. That way the message might finally get through to an industry badly in need of better self-regulation.

how much should I pay?

This just leaves the fifth C – cost. Obviously, it is a personal matter, but you will no doubt hear that one to two months' salary is the norm. There's one point to make about this: it all seems to stem from De Beers' publicity machine. Spend whatever you like and can realistically afford. Remember that De Beers have a near-monopoly of the diamond industry, and that of course, it has an interest in what you spend. And scotch any thoughts that a diamond ring is a sound investment. A retailer can mark up a new diamond ring by up to 100 per cent, and it could lose over half its value the moment you leave the shop. Even with a diamond bought at the virtually wholesale rates of London's jewellery centre, Hatton Garden, it could take more than five years to regain its price. Ignore Jennifer Lopez: love does, in fact, cost a thing.

give her what she wants

It's all well and good knowing your IFs from your I3s, but if you don't buy her the right type of engagement ring, all is lost. Possibly the most important piece of hand-me-down advice is never to surprise her with a diamond ring. Worse still, never buy a ring based on your taste alone. By all means, do all that down-on-one-knee stuff, but she'll warm to you even more if you don't hand her a ring that she will never be comfortable wearing.

One way to find out what she likes is to look at the style of jewellery that's already in her collection. Does she have modern or traditional pieces? Does she favour white gold, yellow gold, two-tone (white and yellow gold) or platinum (currently the most popular for engagement rings)? Also, how does she react to other women's engagement rings? Does she ever express an interest in a style when flicking through fashion magazines? Chances are, however, that after a quick consultation with her girlfriends and female relatives – if you can trust them with your secret – you will glean a fairly accurate picture of her preferred style. (Do you really think it has never been a topic of discussion?) Chances are that it will be a classic diamond solitaire – 76 per cent of all engagement rings are solitaires – but there are many ways to present a single quality stone on a ring. Would she like a Tiffany-style solitaire in which prongs hold the diamond high? Or perhaps a basket setting, or some other low-head style? Without doubt, though, you're best to involve her in your decision-making. It may not match your romantic notion of getting engaged, but she will thank you.

buying from jewellers

There are few alternatives to buying an engagement ring from a jeweller. You could, perhaps, consider buying an antique ring from auction, but if you want a new ring, you're best trudging round as many local jewellers as possible to gauge what's on the market. It's worth remembering that major high-street jewellers are inevitably more pricey than London's jewellery centre at Hatton Garden, so if you can pay a visit there, so much the better. Consider, too, that jewellers are busiest in the run-up to Christmas and before Valentine's Day. August is traditionally their slowest month, so it may be the best time to ask for a better deal.

Post-Ratners, however, jewellers haven't enjoyed the best press, so make sure you run this checklist through your head every time you visit a shop:

* Does this store have a long-standing and solid local reputation?

* Do the staff evidently possess a sound gemmological knowledge? Watch out for gratuitous and unexplained jargon.

* Is the shop willing to sell you diamonds with a well-known gemmological certificate? If so, make sure you keep the original rather than a copy.

* Is the shop a member of a trade association? If so, which one(s)?

* Will the shop present a detailed receipt with your purchase? This is key to any possible insurance claim or future repair.

* Does the shop appear to have a busy repairs service? (A good indication of customer trust.)

* Exactly which warranties and guarantees is the shop offering? Read them closely.

- Will the salesperson let you examine the diamond through a loupe and against a white background? If diamonds are viewed against a black background, the eye's perception of colour is hindered.

from the web

Buying diamond rings via the internet is probably not to be recommended, because you will always want to view the diamonds in person so that you can cover all of the above details. If you do choose to use this method, only ever buy 'cert' stones and pay special attention to the delivery terms and possible tax and duty charges if buying from a foreign-based site. But the internet does offer you the ability to do your homework. These sites [▷] will all let you gauge what styles and prices are currently available:

www.approveddiamonds.com
www.cooldiamonds.com
www.diamonds4u.com
www.diasource.com
www.jewellerywebshop.co.uk
www.mondera.com
www.nydex.com
www.thediamondshop.co.uk
www.theofennell.com

only for the brave

If you are really in the hunt for a good deal, then you could try some of the companies trying to break with the traditional supply chain of the diamond industry. One such company is the mining firm Rex Mining Diamond Corporation, who have set up a website that aims to bypass the retail route and sell wholesale to the public. Its website is **www.rexgems.com**.

Alternatively, try to gain access to the Hatton Garden wholesalers, who normally only sell direct to the retailers. In most cases they will not have any recognizable street presence, just a bell to ring, but will sell loose diamonds up to 50 per cent cheaper than high-street retailers. They won't have time for time-wasters and probably won't be interested in a long sales spiel, but if you know exactly what you're after, give them a try. Contact the jewellery trade associations for names.

PRIMARY RESOURCES

TRADE ASSOCIATIONS

British Jewellers Association
tel: 0121 237 1111
www.bja.org.uk

British Jewellery and Giftware
Federation
tel: 0121 237 1115
www.bjgf.org.uk

The Diamond Information Centre
(sponsored by the Diamond
Trading Company, part of the De
Beers Group)
tel: 020 7404 4444
www.uk.forevermark.com

The Gemmological Association
and Gem Testing Laboratory of
Great Britain
tel: 020 7404 3334
www.gagtl.ac.uk

The Jewellery & Allied Industries
Training Council
tel: 0121 237 1109
www.jaitc.org.uk

The National Association of
Goldsmiths
tel: 020 7613 4445
www.progold.net

DIAMOND CERTIFICATE ISSUERS

American Gem Society (AGS)
tel: 001 702 233 6120
www.agslab.com

Diamond High Council (HRD)
tel: 0032 3 222 05 11
www.diamonds.be

European Gemmological
Laboratory (EGL)
tel: 020 7916 3519
www.egl.co.za

Gemmological Institute of America
Inc (GIA)
tel: 001 760 603 4000
www.gia.org

Independent Gemmological
Laboratories, Inc. (IGL)
tel: 001 212 557 0111

fridges, freezers and washing machines

the basics

Gross symbols of wanton consumerism and wasteful living they may be, but life without white goods – appliances such as fridges, washing machines and dishwashers – is simply unthinkable for the vast majority of us. We will all, at some point, have to face the trip down to the local showroom to talk spin cycles, freezer star ratings and catalytic oven liners, but with an understanding of what to look for and where to shop, it need not be an ordeal and you should even be able to secure a bargain.

The most important consideration, however, should always be what impact that humming lump of metal in your kitchen is going to have on the environment. White goods are justifiably seen as the devil incarnate by environmentalists, who have helped to force the appliance manufacturers to take large strides over the last decade towards cleaning up their act. Even so, there are still good and bad buys when it comes to environmental impact (always look for Energy Efficiency Recommended stickers).

There are also, of course, good and bad buys when it comes to usability, efficiency and convenience. Before you head off on a shopping trip, a good tip is to note down what your energy costs are, as most appliances are rated according to their electricity, water and gas costs per energy unit. Your utility bills will tell you how much each unit costs in your area (electricity, for example, is typically about 6p per kW).

Also note the dimensions of the space awaiting the appliance, down to the nearest millimetre. It may sound obvious, but not all appliances are designed to fit the standard 600 mm × 600 mm kitchen unit spaces. Work out what plumbing you have available (many appliances need a hot water inlet in addition to a cold one), and try to guesstimate the demands of your family: is that stainless-steel designer fridge really going to stand up to the knocks (and mucky fingers) of 2.4 children? Appliances are built to last about ten years, so think hard about what your needs will be in the future.

One important point to remember about white goods (and many other electric consumables) is that despite the seemingly wide range of brand manufacturers on offer, many are owned and built by a relatively small number of bigger parent corporations. What this means for you is that when you find yourself mulling over the merits of two different brands, you could, in fact, just be mulling over the difference in finish: the mechanics inside could be virtually identical. Bosch-Siemens, for example, produce the popular Bosch, Gaggenau, Neff and Siemens brands. If you want to know who produces what, visit **www.transnationale.org/anglais** and take that information with you when researching brands. Always let the sales staff know that you know the difference before they try to sell you a 'better' brand, when another may offer the same features for a lower price.

ovens

Ovens come in many shapes and sizes (ranges, microwaves, eye-level, below-counter, double), but once you have determined the size you need and its location, your decision-making largely centres on functionality and features.

Debates rage as to whether gas or electric ovens rule supreme, but the best combination for a family is normally to have a gas hob, an electric oven and a combination microwave oven (a microwave that can also cook food conventionally). You are unlikely to ever need much more cooking power than this, except for the odd fraught Christmas dinner.

Features for which you will end up praising a higher being – known to many simply as Delia – include a glass door that won't burn a child's hands, an interior light, an internal fan for more even cooking, a shelf rack that lets you pull out more than one shelf at a time, an advanced clock and timer, a bottom- (rather than side-) hinged door that is strong enough, when lowered, to let you rest hot trays and dishes on it, and a self-cleaning function. Anything beyond these features is likely to be used as much as your chef's blowtorch and vegetable juicer lying idle at the back of a cupboard.

With self-cleaning, look for buzzwords such as catalytic liner and pyrolysis. Both of these features let you crank up the oven's temperature to maximum in order to burn away any grease and stains that may have built up after all those roasts and melted cheese dishes we love to cook. Each clean will cost about 20p in electricity costs – a lot cheaper and, arguably, environmentally sounder than a spray can of chemical oven cleaner.

Don't forget the costs of installing an oven. If it needs a gas supply, it is required by law to be connected by a member of the Council for Registered Gas Installers (CORGI). Electric oven installations aren't governed so strictly, but it is recommended that you hire a member of the National Inspection Council for Electrical Installation Contractors (NICEIC).

Microwave ovens just need to be plugged in, but make sure you get one with adequate wattage. If, like most people, you just use a microwave for defrosting food and heating up the odd drink or ready-prepared meal, don't waste money on unnecessary features. Spend any extra on getting a 1,000-watt oven, which will boil a mug of water in a minute, compared to a 600-watt one, which will take up to two minutes and twenty seconds to perform the same task.

washing machines and dryers

Washing machines can cost anywhere between £200 and £1,000, but most people will be satisfied by one that costs between £300 and £600. For this, you will get a machine that can handle 5 kg to 6 kg loads (adequate for an average family) and a high spin speed (1,100 rpm or more), which will ultimately pay for itself by reducing any drying costs.

When it comes to features, 'fuzzy logic' is your first goal. This is the computerized 'brain' inside a machine that helps to maximize its efficiency. Fuzzy logic should help to increase the machine's spin performance, too. Look for an efficiency of between A and C on the energy-rating label.

The settings you require will be a personal choice depending on the variety of your clothes and linen, but most people rarely stray from the intensive, economy, delicate and half-load settings. Modern detergents mean that pre-wash cycles are of little benefit. Guard yourself, too, against the meaningless jargon so beloved by manufacturers, such as Aquatonic Wash and Bioprofile: they're just fancy names for common features.

American-style top loaders have become more popular in recent years, but are far from economical in comparison with a more traditional European-style front loader. A front loader will use about 25 gallons per wash, compared to the top loader's 45-gallon thirst. Front loaders also spin and wash much more efficiently.

When you're considering a dryer, the main feature that is worth paying for is a moisture-sensor. This will save energy by stopping the drying cycle as soon as it detects the load is dry. It will also stop the cycle slightly earlier if you want your clothes 'iron dry'.

Space restrictions lead many people to opt for a washer-dryer. However convenient, they are rarely more economical than two separate machines. If you are restricted simply by a lack of venting space for your dryer, perhaps consider buying the more expensive condenser dryers, which let all the water build up in a tray or be pumped away, instead of it evaporating via a vent.

dishwashers

Nearly half of all households now have a dishwasher. The common myth is that they are an additional blight on the environment, but ignoring the issue of the machine's disposal and manufacture, washing your dishes in a machine is far cheaper in energy and water costs than washing by hand (and unchains you from the kitchen sink). Each machine wash will cost about 9p compared to the 20p it will cost to wash your dishes by hand. A machine will also save a family about three hundred hours a year in time bent over the sink. And it will wash your dishes more hygienically, too.

The things to remember when choosing a dishwasher are much the same as when choosing a washing machine. Always check for energy efficiency ratings and don't overdo it on the range of cycles. All you will ever need are the rinse, economy, regular and heavy-duty cycles.

A good feature to seek is a timer. By setting your dishwasher to come on in the middle of the night, you can benefit from cheaper electricity rates that are sometimes offered by energy firms. If it's an issue for you, ask how loud the dishwasher is when operating. As a guide, a boiling kettle registers at about fifty decibels.

fridges and freezers

Your refrigerator is the only appliance that will be plugged in and left on for its entire life. It is therefore a major energy guzzler, and has the dubious distinction of also needing those wicked refrigerants that we are told do so much harm to the ozone layer.

For these very reasons it is important to find the right-sized fridge for your needs. There has been a worrying trend in the last few years for us to buy big trendy American-style fridges. Just like the ridiculously huge people carriers and four-wheel drives that are used for the suburban school run, we are moving towards the use of fridges with excessive capacity. On the other hand, an over-packed, small fridge is highly inefficient, as the cool air cannot circulate, with the result that it uses more energy.

A good way of working out how much capacity you need is to remember that an average family – with all its bottles of pop, tubs of marge and cartons of juice – will get by with 18 cubic feet of fridge space. That family will need about half that amount in freezer space, too.

The best option is to get a fridge-freezer that has its freezer compartment at the bottom. Cold air sinks, and in the long run, it will be more economical than one with its freezer at the top. And an eye-level fridge compartment is more convenient too.

Try to avoid gadgets such as ice dispensers and water coolers located in the fridge door. There's not much inside a fridge that can go wrong, but gadgets like these will only increase the need for repairs in the future. Two features that are worth looking out for, though, are dual temperature control and automatic defrost. These let you adjust the fridge and freezer temperatures separately or automatically – which is good if you want to stop your fridge from frosting up.

When comparing fridges, go for ones that have the most flexible shelves. You want to be able to clean and move them around easily. Some even let you alter the height without emptying the fridge, via clever adjustable shelves. Transparent freezer compartments are good too, as they let you find what you're looking for quickly, thus preventing you from leaving the door open for ages while you rummage around behind the frozen peas for that ready meal. And if you are likely to be moving home, you want to invest in reversible

ethics watch

Ethical Consumer magazine says that all fridges and freezers use coolant gases in order to work, such as HFCs (hydrofluorocarbons). Although HFCs don't destroy the ozone layer like their predecessors CFCs and HCFCs, they have a high global warming potential. It advises buying an appliance that uses the R600a hydrocarbon coolant, a mixture of propane and butane. And taking into account the records of the manufacturers on a range of social, environmental and animal welfare issues, the magazine's Best Buy advice was to choose Miele's A-rated appliances and Servis's A-rated M7604 model.

When the magazine last published research into washing machines, one of the main issues addressed was the corporate interests of some of the major manufacturers. Attracting attention was Electrolux, part of the Wallenburg family empire embracing AstraZeneca (genetic engineering and pesticides), ABB (controversial dams in the developing world) and Stora Enso (logging of old growth forests). Taking into account the records of the producers on a range of social, environmental and animal welfare issues, *Ethical Consumer*'s overall Best Buys were the Asko W620 and Hoover Quattro AE 240.

The magazine's main recommendations for people choosing ovens were to choose gas rather than electric appliances where possible. As currently generated, electricity produces three times the carbon dioxide emissions of natural gas for the same amount of heat. Taking into account the records of the producers on a range of social and environmental issues, *Ethical Consumer*'s overall oven Best Buys were Atag, Homark, Stoves and Valor.

Many of the manufacturers of white goods, such as Bosch, Siemens and Electrolux, were also cited by the magazine as having defence or civil nuclear contracts, or subsidiaries operating in oppressive regimes.

For more information, visit www.ethicalconsumer.org or call 0161 226 2929.

doors, as you don't yet know what the layout of your new kitchen might be.

making your purchase

Most of us only know one option when it comes to buying white goods – the high street. While it is always great to see the goods in person, the best deals are probably to be found online nowadays. It may seem a bit daunting buying something as large as a fridge-freezer via a website, but stick to the bigger, well-known firms (see 'primary resources') and you should be fine. As ever, explore both options to hunt down the best prices.

Whether you opt for the high street or the website, you need the same questions answered:

- Are they an authorized dealer for the brand you want?
- How much are the delivery costs?
- Are the delivery times flexible and precise, or do you have to take a day off work in order to be at home when they deign to deliver?
- Will you be compensated if the delivery is delayed?
- Will they take away your old appliance and dispose of it responsibly? (Remember that most councils will dispose of white goods free of charge.)
- What are the precise terms of any finance deal the firm may be offering? Beware 'buy now, pay later' and interest-free period deals that charge high interest if you miss the first payments.

You will almost inevitably be pestered to buy an extended warranty, especially if you plump for a high-street retailer. They are always best avoided due to the excessive profit margin they give to the retailer, and in any case, you almost always get a year's guarantee from the manufacturer – the time when most repairs are needed.

There are, however, alternatives to buying from the high street or a website. First, there are the clearance sales and auctions, where some of the big retailers offload 'cosmetically damaged' stock or stock that has been previously sold. All, however, are still under the manufacturer's year-long guarantee. Comet, the large high-street chain, holds such auctions on a dedicated website (**www.clearance-comet.co.uk**) and the kitchen-fitting firm Magnet holds clearance sales at its industrial park outlet sites (see 'primary resources'). It's also worth looking on **www.letsbuyit.co.uk**, the co-buying shop that lowers the price on goods as more and more people place orders. With all these options, double-check before committing to make sure that other retailers aren't more competitive. Don't assume their prices are unbeatable.

If you fancy buying a second-hand appliance, you should contact the Furniture Recycling Network, which reconditions old appliances. As 600,000 appliances are discarded every year in the UK, with only 100,000 being recycled, it is certainly worth investigating. If considering other recyclers, stick to ones accredited by the Industry Council for Electrical Equipment Recycling (ICER).

PRIMARY RESOURCES

HIGH-STREET RETAILERS

Argos
tel: 0870 909 1110
www.argos.co.uk

Allders
tel: 0845 234 0139
www.allders.com

Comet
tel: 0845 600 7002
www.comet.co.uk

Co-op
tel: 0161 437 3078
www.electrical.coop.co.uk

Currys
tel: 0870 1545 570
www.currys.co.uk

Debenhams
tel: 020 7580 3000
www.debenhams.com

House of Fraser
tel: 020 7529 4700
www.houseoffraser.co.uk

John Lewis
tel: 08456 049049
www.johnlewis.com

Littlewoods
tel: 0845 757 3457
www.littlewoodsextra.com

STOCK CLEARANCE OUTLETS

Comet auctions
tel: 0845 600 7002
www.clearance-comet.co.uk

Magnet clearance outlets (located at Keighley, Birmingham and Darlington)
tel: 01535 680461
0121 327 3201
01642 344564
www.magnet.co.uk

LEADING ONLINE RETAILERS

www.applianceonline.co.uk
www.bedirect.co.uk
www.electricshop.com
www.hutchisonsdirect.co.uk
www.qed-uk.com
www.tesco.com/electrical
www.trade-appliances.co.uk
www.unbeatable.co.uk
www.we-sell-it.co.uk

RECYCLING ORGANIZATIONS

Furniture Recycling Network
tel: 0116 254 4189

Industry Council For Electronic Equipment Recycling
tel: 020 7729 4766
www.icer.org.uk

MANUFACTURERS

AEG
tel: 08705 350350
www.aeg.co.uk

Ariston
tel: 08700 104305
www.merloni.com

Beko
tel: 01923 818121
www.beko.co.uk

Belling
tel: 01162 123456
www.belling.co.uk

Bosch
tel: 0870 727 0446
www.boschappliances.co.uk

Brandt
tel: 01256 308000,
http://uk.brandt.com

Creda
tel: 08701 546474
www.creda.co.uk

Daewoo
tel: 01189 252500
www.daewoo-electronics.co.uk

Delonghi
tel: 0845 600 6845
www.delonghi.co.uk

Elcold
tel: 01606 888962
www.elcold.com

Electrolux
tel: 01635 572700
www.electrolux.co.uk

Haier
tel: 01527 578333

Hinari
tel: 020 8787 3111

Hoover
tel: 01685 721222
www.hoover.co.uk

Hotpoint
tel: 0870 150 6070
www.hotpoint.co.uk

Indesit
tel: 08700 104309
www.merloni.com

Lec
tel: 01243 863161
www.lec.co.uk

LG
tel: 0870 607 5544
www.lgelectronics.co.uk

Liebherr
tel: 01977 665665
www.liebherr.com/us

Miele
tel: 01235 554455
www.miele.co.uk

Neff
tel: 0870 240 0080
www.neff.co.uk

Norfrost
01847 821333
www.norfrost.co.uk

Panasonic
tel: 08705 357357
www.panasonic.co.uk

Samsung
tel: 020 8391 0168
www.samsungelectronics.co.uk

Sanyo
tel: 01923 246363
www.sanyo.co.uk

Sharp
tel: 0800 262958
www.sharp.co.uk

Siemens
tel: 0870 240 0070
www.siemensappliances.co.uk

Skandiluxe
tel: 020 8951 3711

Vestfrost
tel: 01844 352906
www.vestfrost.com

Whirlpool
tel: 0870 600 8989
www.whirlpool.co.uk

Zanussi
tel: 0870 572 7727
www.zanussi.co.uk

furniture, fixtures and fittings

the basics

And you thought buying your home was the hard bit... Well, now you've got to go out there and furnish it.

The novelty of sitting on an unpacked tea crate cradling a mug of tea while lovingly staring at the four bare walls around you will soon wear off when all you want to do is draw the curtains, light the fire, then walk across a warm carpet and just kick back onto a sofa.

Most of us shiver with fear at the thought of bedecking our home with furniture, fixtures and fittings. It all looks nice and simple when the interior decorators work their magic on TV, but when we are faced with choosing sofas, finding curtains or fitting carpets, we collectively reach for the headache pills.

Things aren't helped by the fact that the home furnishings industry has a poor reputation for customer service. We've heard it all before: late deliveries, mistaken orders, misleading price offers, poor quality goods. So, how can we guard ourselves from the rogues and bad craftsmen, and still get a good deal?

Even though taste and budget will lead us all in different directions, the basic buying rules still apply: do your research, shop prepared, shop around and shop for details.

Most of us have a good sense of the style and fashions we like when it comes to furnishings. Whether other people will agree with you is open to debate – we are all style snobs, after all – but you should broaden your style radar before any big purchase by mugging up on what's available in the interiors magazines, newspaper style pages, the myriad home interiors TV programmes, or even the interior shows such as the Ideal Home Exhibition. You will also soon gauge who are the most recommended and trusted retailers.

When you do head for the shops, take as much information about your home with you as possible. Take measurements of, for example, your doors, floor space and window frames, in addition to a tape measure and samples of your wallpaper, carpet or paint colour. All of these will help you to decide whether something you have your eye on will be right for your home.

As you begin your search, make sure you enquire about the conditions of delivery and any installation costs. There's a reason why shops like IKEA are so popular: even though you may have to battle with the crowds, at least you know that you can take most items home with you that day. Also, prices at shops that offer self-assembly furniture are between 25 and 50 per cent cheaper than retailers selling finished furniture.

A wait of four to eight weeks from the day of ordering is typical with furnishing stores, as many products are made to order. You must obtain delivery dates in writing if you are to have any redress in the event of any delay. At the same time, get a quote (or receipt, if you're buying) detailing everything from the price, colour and material to the product type. If you're buying carpet, for example, you will want to go even further, and secure, in writing, the exact fitting dimensions, the price per metre, how much underlay is required, the underlay's cost, the fitting fee, colour and product codes, guarantees and proof that the carpet meets flammability standards.

Lastly, it is unwise to throw away anything before its replacement has arrived, as anyone who has been let down by one of those 'Pre-Xmas Delivery Guaranteed' offers will testify.

furniture

Dining tables, armchairs, side cabinets, armoires, sofas, occasional tables, chests – advising on how to buy every piece of furniture available would fill a book, but by taking one example, the sofa, a good set of basic principles can be established that should be remembered when shopping for any piece of furniture.

A sofa is likely to be one of the most expensive pieces of furniture you will ever buy. As it is typically made up of a wooden frame, padding and a material covering, a sofa throws up most of the questions about the quality of construction that are raised when buying most types of furniture.

When you head round the shops, don't forget that your tired legs will make every sofa you sit in feel in some way comfortable. For this reason, you ideally want to spend ten minutes with each sofa you test. If you like to slob out at home on the sofa, do so in the shop. Ignoring fellow-shoppers, lie back and try to get really comfortable.

Once you are happy with the ergonomics, begin to test the construction. Feel all around the sofa for the frame with your hands. A good sign of a poorly made sofa is if the covering material touches the inner frame at any point. Padding should come between them everywhere. If not, the material will wear through much faster. Look at the stitching and the number of inner springs or webbed slats (the more the merrier). Listen for creaks and squeaks. A frame constructed with nails and glue is a lot weaker than one held together by screws or proper carpentry joints.

If shopping with a friend (always best), both of you should sit apart and see if the sofa pushes you towards the middle. Sofas shouldn't be so comfortable that you sink right into their centre. Anything more than a 10-centimetre sag and you could start to get back pains. For the same reason, they shouldn't be too deep either.

Beyond the comfort of a sofa, most people are more concerned about the style and quality of the covering material. Various materials are available: cotton, flax/linen, wool, silk, leather, acetate, acrylic, olefin, nylon, satin, damask or a blend of any of these. Clearly, it's a personal choice, as are the pattern and colour, but the quality is what you need to concentrate on.

Most shops will offer you a good selection, but try to get as many samples and swatches of material as you can. Many shops offer sofa frames of a standard construction: the standout factor is always the material, so gather samples as you go round the shops. You can even add to these by sending off for more from mail-order or internet fabric retailers (try **www.fabricsdirect.co.uk** or **www.findafabric.com** for starters).

If a shop won't consider material that you have found elsewhere (many will not), you could try to find a local upholsterer who will help you. Possibly the cheapest way to do this is to find an old sofa – could your old sofa be given a new lease of life by being re-upholstered? – and then contact the Association of Master Upholsterers & Soft Furnishers to find reputable local help. As a general guide, a two-seater sofa will require between 10 and 14 metres of material, whereas a three-seater will need 12 to 18 metres.

Whatever material you use, it must meet legal flammability standards. When buying new, this should be a given, but remember this if you are re-upholstering any old furniture. Furniture shops often place a lot of emphasis on offering you a stain-repellent treatment. You have to ask yourself whether the extra cost – up to £200 – is really worth it. The only stain-repellent that is truly effective is one that has been part of the manufacturing process. Any post-factory spray-based treatment will offer questionable protection. Just make sure you buy furniture with fabric that is suitable to your lifestyle (and your children's). Look for washing instructions. Is it dry-clean-only or can covers be removed? Remember that zips on cushions do not always mean they can be machine-washed, so read the labels carefully.

When buying furniture other than a sofa, apply the same basic checklists before you buy. Research all materials used: don't be misled, for example, by veneer and imitation leather. Make sure sales staff explain everything in detail. Inspect construction techniques vigorously, and yes, slide any drawers in and out to check for a smooth action.

curtains and blinds

Another major expense when furnishing your home, curtains and blinds can be an important focal point and statement within any room. You can, of course, buy off-the-peg 'window treatments', as they are known in the trade, from a shop, but many people choose or need to have curtains and blinds tailor-made to fit a particular window.

Your first port of call should be second-hand curtain-sellers, as even after having them professionally cleaned, you will be saving hundreds of pounds on a comparable pair tailor-made for you. Try your local Curtain Exchange first (tel: 020 7731 8316 for details).

If you do want to have your own pair made, research the fabrics just as you would for a sofa, by collecting and sending off for as many samples as you can. Retailers such as Swatchbox (**www.swatchbox.co.uk**), Prêt à Vivre (**www.pretavivre.com**) and Web-blinds (**www.web-blinds.com**) will send you free samples to help you choose your made-to-measure curtains or blinds.

carpets and flooring

The simplest way to convey the pitfalls of buying a carpet is to quote the 'seven truths' spelled out by a large US retailer.

1. There is no such thing as 'free' labour.
2. There is no such thing as an 'invisible' seam.
3. There is no such thing as a stain-proof carpet.
4. There is no such thing as a 'miracle' fibre.
5. There is no such thing as a real '70 per cent off'.
6. The life of a carpet depends on your lifestyle – read the warranty.
7. Installation is everything.

Begin your trawl for a retailer by checking **www.carpet-index.com** and **www.carpetinfo.co.uk**. Both offer reams of advice about buying carpets and directories of retailers.

When you have a list of target shops, follow the same advice as when buying curtains: collect as many samples as you can and take them home to compare and contrast. (Very competitive prices and samples can be found online at retailers such as **www.ukcarpetsdirect.com**.) You will soon notice that beyond colour and pattern, the material types offered are quite varied. As well as having a choice between materials such as wool, nylon, olefin, acrylic and polyester, you will also have a choice of fibre density (amount of fibre per square inch), pile (height of fibre) and texture (the style in which the fibre is looped, twisted or cut).

Beyond any preferred style considerations, ask the sales staff about issues such as 'pile reversal' and carpet protection treatments. Pile reversal – when a carpet looks as if it has been shaded or water-stained – is often seen by customers as a fault, and one they often don't spot until installation. Upon inspection, it is simply a case of the pile being brushed in a different direction, but many customers complain about it. Although it isn't considered a fault by manufacturers or industry trade associations, make sure you have been made aware of it before you commit yourself after seeing just a sample.

As with sofas, protection treatments should be applied as part of the manufacturing process and not really be offered as part of the sales patter. Any spray-on treatment will be of questionable quality and unquestionable extra expense. And when you're going over the conditions of the carpet's warranty, pay particular attention to the small print about stains. It is common for the warranty to exclude any stain other than those made by food or beverage spills. You may even find some foods being excluded, too, such as mustard or herbal teas, due to their high natural dye content. Additional exclusions could include carpet used in high-traffic areas such as stairs or by front doors. Some warranties demand that professional carpet cleaners are always used and that you contact the manufacturer or retailer within thirty days of the spill.

When it comes to fitting a carpet, make sure you get a member of the National Institute of Carpet and Floorlayers. A good fitter will make a huge difference to the final appearance. They will know how important the underlay is, and how it adds to the life of the carpet.

Of course, dozens of other options are available to you for covering a floor – seagrass, coir, tiles, stripped floorboards, linoleum, laminates – but whatever you choose, make sure you find the highest-quality fitter. Remember: installation is everything.

fireplaces

We are all familiar with the perception that a quality fireplace is one of the key attractions when choosing a home, but unless you are fortunate enough to have an older property with its original fireplaces still in place, you will have to begin the search for something appropriate.

It seems that it is always others who have the good fortune to find a fireplace in a skip, so reclamation yards – check the Yellow Pages, **www.yell.com** or **www.salvo.co.uk** – are always a good place to start, especially if you live in a period house and feel that the fireplaces on offer in most shops may not be suitable.

Alternatively, get hold of the National Fireplace Association's yearbook (visit **www.nfa.org.uk** for details). It lists everything you need to know about choosing and finding a new fireplace. You could also add an online trawl to your research tick-list. Online retailers such as **www.fireplacedirect.co.uk** will give you a quick guide to how much different styles cost.

lighting

Three types of lighting are used to illuminate homes: ambient light, task lighting and display lighting. Ambient lighting typically consists of a ceiling-mounted bulb and shade that fills the entire room with a constant light. Task lighting is things like desk lamps and standard lamps, which focus light onto desks, tables and walls, and in so doing help to produce more light contrast in the room. Display lighting purposefully highlights an object like a painting.

The style of lighting is a highly personal choice, but contact the Lighting Association (see 'primary resources') if you need help making a list of local retailers and specialists. If you choose to buy second-hand fittings, make sure a professional checks that the wiring meets safety regulations, and whatever fitting you choose, get an electrician to install it. This is never something to be left for DIY Sunday.

If at all possible, however, lighting should be planned when a property is rewired, as you will want to make sure the switches and fittings are all located properly.

making your purchase

The vast majority of us head off to the giant specialist superstores such as Courts, DFS, IKEA and Furniture Village when we want furniture. The high-street retailers and department stores such as Heal's, Habitat, John Lewis, and Marks & Spencer are also extremely popular. It's easy to see why: they're car- and family-friendly (in most cases), are a known name (important for people nervous about making a big purchase), and in most cases are perceived as offering good value.

While all of this is true in many ways, furniture retailers do have a poor reputation when it comes to delivery, so – as has already been pointed out – pay close attention to the terms and conditions. Watch out for the classic 'bait and switch' offer, particularly at sale time. Carpet retailers, in particular, are known for the dubious tactic of luring the customer in with an enticing advert, only for the offer to have miraculously sold out or ended.

There are, however, many other ways to purchase furniture. New furniture can be purchased online or through mail-order catalogues, both of which are becoming more popular, as they usually offer more competitive prices than the high street. For a list of mail-order furniture retailers, visit **www.catalink.co.uk**, and for an example of popular online furniture retailers visit **www.furniture123.co.uk**. Most of the main high-street stores also now offer home delivery through the internet or mail order.

There is, of course, a whole world of antique and second-hand furniture, fixtures and fittings out there. Every town, it seems, has at least a handful of antique shops or an auction house, but the real bargains are to be had where the dealers themselves get their stock – the salvage yards, and in particular, the large trade fairs.

Europe's largest fair is held at Newark racecourse six times a year (visit **www.newarkantiquesfair.com** for details). If you get there early along with the traders, you can find some incredible bargains. But take cash – this isn't a chequebook or credit-card environment. Numerous other fairs take place around the country. For a full list, get hold of a trade publication, such as *Antiques Trade Gazette* or the *Antique Dealer Newspaper*.

ethics watch

The manufacturing process used to make carpets is particularly harmful to the environment. As carpet trimmings can be sold on to recycling plants and used in a variety of ways, ask the retailer if it or the manufacturer operates a policy of passing on unwanted carpet to recyclers.

Ethical Consumer magazine also recommends buying the *Green Directory*, available from WH Smith, as it lists a number of small businesses that can supply off-the-peg, as well as made-to-order furniture.

For people looking for new items, the magazine says it is always worth thinking about the construction materials used. Natural fabrics and stuffing are best, and wood labelled with the Forestry Stewardship Council (FSC) logo is guaranteed to come from sustainably managed sources.

In larger stores, customers could enquire whether the company has a code of conduct for workers' rights in subcontractor factories, and where specific pieces of furniture were made.

For more information, visit www.ethicalconsumer.org or call 0161 226 2929.

Many dealers also head to France for even better deals. Paris has a handful of good fairs, but perhaps the best one for well-priced furniture is the flea market at Porte de Montreuil held on Sundays (the Puces de St-Ouen, otherwise known as Clignancourt, used to be good for bargains, but is now probably too much of a tourist trap). When in France, also look out for posters and signs bearing the word 'brocante', as they imply that someone is selling antiques and bric-a-brac close by.

Good architectural reclamation yards are, sadly, a bit thin on the ground, and sellers are also increasingly aware of the true worth of fashionable items, given the current home-decorating craze. However, they're certainly worth exploring. For a good list of yards around the UK, visit **www.periodproperty.co.uk** (select 'Architectural Salvage' in the 'Seeking Specialists' section).

expert view

Matthew Line, editor of *Homes & Gardens*, says you should remember the following points:

* Be very clear about your needs. Write a list to take with you when buying a piece. What do you want it to do?

* Look at pieces in natural daylight. Ask for them to be taken near the window. It could make the world of difference.

* Consider furniture as part of the bone structure of a room before you start purchasing accessories.

* Look at magazines that emulate your style, as these will give you a source book that is tailored to you.

* Treat furniture in your home as you would if you were dressing yourself, i.e. mix designer with high street.

* Buy pieces that fit both your style and needs, and you'll find you won't end up with redundant pieces.

* Don't forget lighting. You can change the whole atmosphere of a room by dividing the central light-source into three or four lamps placed around it. Also try changing the bulbs to a different wattage to create focal points.

PRIMARY RESOURCES

INTERIOR DESIGN AND TRADE MAGAZINES

Antique Dealer Newspaper
tel: 0870 607 2301
www.dmgworldmedia.com

Antiques Diary
tel: 0118 940 2165
www.antiquesworld.co.uk/
antiquesdiary.html

Antiques Trade Gazette
tel: 020 7420 6601
www.antiquestradegazette.com

25 Beautiful Homes
tel: 020 7261 5000
www.ipcmedia.com

Country Homes and Interiors
tel: 020 7261 6451
www.ipcmedia.com

Country Living
tel: 020 7439 5000
www.countryliving.co.uk

Elle Decoration
tel: 020 7437 9011
www.emapmagazines.co.uk

Home & Country
tel: 020 7731 5777
www.womens-institute.co.uk/
maga.shtml

Homes & Antiques
tel: 020 8576 2000
www.beeb.com/homesandantiques

Homes & Gardens
tel: 020 7261 5678
www.ipcmedia.com

Homes & Ideas
tel: 020 7261 6474
www.ipcmedia.com

Homestyle
tel: 020 7928 5869

House and Garden
tel: 020 7499 9080
www.houseandgarden.co.uk

House Beautiful
tel: 020 7439 5000
www.housebeautiful.co.uk

Ideal Home
tel: 020 7261 6474
www.ipcmedia.com

Living Etc
tel: 020 7261 5000
www.ipcmedia.com

The Real Homes Magazine
tel: 020 7554 5700
www.cabalcomm.com

Wallpaper*
tel: 020 7322 1177
www.wallpaper.com

World of Interiors
tel: 020 7499 9080
www.worldofinteriors.co.uk

Your Home
tel: 020 7519 5798
www.yourhomemagazine.co.uk

TRADE ASSOCIATIONS

Association of British Furniture Manufacturers
tel: 020 7724 0851
www.bfm.org.uk

Association of Master Upholsterers & Soft Furnishers
tel: 01633 215454
www.upholsterers.co.uk

British Carpet Manufacturers Association
tel: 01562 747351

Contract Flooring Association
tel: 0115 941 1126
www.cfa.org.uk

Furniture Industry Research Association
tel: 01438 777700
www.fira.co.uk

Lighting Association
tel: 01952 290905
www.lightingassociation.com

Lighting Industry Federation
tel: 020 8675 5432
www.lif.co.uk

National Fireplace Association
tel: 0121 200 1310
www.nfa.org.uk

National Institute of Carpet and Floorlayers
tel: 0115 958 3077
www.nicf.carpetinfo.co.uk

HIGH-STREET RETAILERS

Allders
tel: 0845 234 0139
www.allders.com

Carpet Right
tel: 020 8568 9865
www.carpetright.co.uk

Conran
tel: 0870 600 1232
www.conran.co.uk

Cotswold Company
tel: 0870 550 2233
www.cotswoldco.com

Courts
tel: 020 8640 3322
www.courts.co.uk

Debenhams
tel: 0845 6055 044
www.debenhams.com

DFS
tel: 020 8688 0083
www.dfs-online.co.uk

Furniture Village
tel: 020 7387 7000
www.furniturevillage.co.uk

Futon Company
tel: 0845 609 4455
www.futoncompany.co.uk

Habitat
tel: 020 7631 3880
www.habitat.co.uk

Heal's
tel: 020 7636 1666
www.heals.co.uk

IKEA
tel: 020 8208 5600
www.ikea.co.uk

John Lewis
tel: 020 7629 7711
www.johnlewis.com

Marks & Spencer
tel: 020 7268 1234
www.marksandspencer.com

MFI
tel: 0800 028 0937
www.mfi.co.uk

Sofa Workshop
tel: 01798 343400
www.sofaworkshop.co.uk

Viva Sofa
tel: 01443 239444
www.vivasofa.co.uk

LARGE TRADE FAIRS AND EXHIBITIONS

Ideal Home Exhibition (held at Earl's Court, London, in March and at Glasgow during October)
www.idealhomeshow.co.uk

Olympia Fine Art and Antiques (high-end fair held in London three times a year)
tel: 0870 736 3105
www.olympia-antiques.com

For details on additional large outdoor antique trade fairs, such as Newark and Ardingly, visit
www.dmgworldmedia.com/corporate/products.asp?type=ce

gym memberships

the basics

You can't argue with the statistics: 70 per cent of men and 80 per cent of women don't get enough exercise. This doesn't mean running marathons or pumping iron: it means that most of us are not even doing the thirty minutes a day of 'brisk walking' that health professionals say we should be doing five days a week in order to stay healthy.

Our sedentary modern lifestyle largely consists of sleeping, eating, commuting, working, eating, working, commuting, eating, sleeping – in that order. Add the fact that we are becoming ever more deskbound at work and that not enough of us eat our recommended daily intake of five helpings of fresh fruit and veg, and you can see where we're going collectively wrong.

The modern answer to this has been either to crack open a beer, grab the remote and deal with it tomorrow, or to bite the bullet and sign up at a gym. Since 1996, according to the Fitness Industry Association (FIA), there has been a 25 per cent increase in the number of gyms and health clubs in the UK. That means there are over 2,600 such establishments all vying for your signature. Such is the demand that about 18 per cent of us – 8.6 million – are now signed-up gym members. That's a 4 per cent rise in the last two years. It seems the days of buying a mail-order fitness bike for the spare bedroom, only to see it miraculously turn into an unwieldy coat hook, are thankfully over.

However, the ever-present problem with joining a gym is retention. How many of us have promised ourselves a healthy New Year after two weeks of death by turkey over Christmas, only to be frightened off going to the gym by one chilly morning or a missed episode of *EastEnders*? A quarter of us drop out of going to the gym six months after signing up. That figure grows to 40 per cent after a year. Reasons cited include 'can't afford the fees', 'overcrowding', 'I moved' – and yes, 'I lost motivation'.

So if you're considering joining a gym, make sure that you keep asking this simple question: will this gym and its staff keep me motivated?

what do you really want from the gym?

Although most gyms appear to look the same from the outside, there are many different services that a gym can offer. Do you want a posey gym in which to show off your future pecs or abs? Do you want a gym that hosts varied classes, such as aerobics, Pilates and yoga? Are you looking for one that has a vibrant social scene, or do you want to keep your head down and just get on with shedding some pounds in peace? Perhaps you are just concerned that the staff will provide you with enough motivation and encouragement. All of these questions must be answered by your initial research.

But before you head off to the nearest local gyms, have you considered all your options? As well as member-only gyms, you always have your local authority leisure centre. Most hold classes and have gyms, as well as a pool. Would this suit your needs? At the very least, go and check it out and see what it has to offer. After all, it could save you hundreds of pounds.

At the other end of the scale are the health clubs. Even more expensive than gyms, health clubs tend to concentrate on pampering their clients with treatments such as massage, tanning, spas and so on, rather than just the circuit training and exercise machines. They will also offer much more comfortable surroundings, such as changing rooms.

Alternatively, many people are now opting for personal trainers. It may sound horribly Hollywood, but the principal draw of a personal trainer is that they act as a professional nag. They can also, if you're willing to pay, adapt to your schedule – ideal for the time-poor.

Whichever option you go for, you should expect to pay – a lot. An average gym membership costs in the region of £20 to £40 a month, depending on location and facilities. On top of that is the usual sign-up fee, which can vary enormously, but can easily top £100. Join a trendy, city-centre gym and the prices can rocket. For example, the Chelsea Harbour Club in London, best known as Princess Diana's exercise haunt, costs about £150 a month. Add the £2,900 sign-up fee and you have got a bill of nearly £5,000 in your first year – and that's if they accept you as a member. An extreme example, perhaps, but an indication of how much money getting fit can cost.

Don't forget the extras, too. The towel hire, the locker deposit, the juice bar, the extra classes, the racquet hire: there are many ways for a gym to earn more money from you. And you haven't bought that essential pair of quality trainers yet, have you?

choosing your gym

The first exercise for your underused 206 bones and 600-plus muscles is to set out on foot and visit your local gyms – at least three. You can easily find where the nearest ones are located by typing your postcode into one of the gym search websites (see 'primary resources').

When choosing a gym, the first rule is to make sure that it is within ten minutes of your home or workplace. Any further away and the ability to drum up continued enthusiasm will fade faster than a love handle after a week on the rowing machine. If you don't live in a large town or city, it is unlikely that you will have three gyms within ten minutes of you, but do try and visit as many as you can to make sure you have an accurate gauge of the standards and services available in your area.

The other principal rule is to take along a friend. Other than acting as a valuable second opinion, you might be able to convince them to join with you. As well as the fact that partners, for example, often get a cheaper deal if they get joint membership, you can also nag each other when your motivation slips.

Before calling in on a gym, ring them to see if you can book a good time for a walk-round with one of the instructors. Gyms are normally busiest between 5 and 7pm on weekdays. Although you do want to see the gym in action at a time when you might be attending, you will first want to view all the facilities without sweaty people constantly pushing past you. It's only on your second visit – never sign up after just one – that you should view it when at its busiest.

If finding a parking space is important to you, have a quick look at the car park to see how busy it is before stepping through the doors. Your radar should immediately be set to detecting the general atmosphere of the gym: is it busy? do the instructors look busy? is there loud music playing? does it smell fresh or stale? When the instructor meets you, they will normally get straight into their sales patter, something that they will go through dozens of times a week. Try to lead the conversation as you are shown round, rather than just letting them keep talking about how great the gym is and why it would make sense for you to become a member – that is their job, after all. There are many key questions you need answered on your first visit. Here are some of the most important:

- How many members do they have and what is the membership ceiling? Ask for the square footage of the gym. The ideal ratio of square footage to members is between 10:1 and 15:1. Any less and it is likely to be overcrowded.

- Is the gym accredited by the FIA? If it is, it should have a plaque on display somewhere in reception and will have signed up to the association's code of practice. The best clubs are presented with FLAME (Fitness Leadership and Management Excellence) awards.

- Are the instructors properly trained and members of the FIA's Register of Exercise Professionals? Are they also trained in first aid?

- Are new members properly screened for health problems? They should be asking you about back and heart problems, in particular. They should also keep members' progress records and be regularly assessing you.

- How long do members have to wait for machines and equipment at peak periods? To get an honest answer, try and collar a member by stopping for a drink at the club's cafe or drinks machine. Don't miss this opportunity to ask them about the gym's general vibe and level of professionalism.

* Is there a drinking-water fountain near the exercising equipment and studios? Are the rooms well lit and fully air-conditioned?

* Do the staff constantly monitor all the areas, and do they look attentive? Look out for instructors and staff loitering at reception chatting. Shouldn't they be somewhere else?

* Are safety rules and instructions displayed by all the equipment? Do they keep up with the latest advances and fitness science? And how old is the present equipment?

* What are the changing rooms like? Are they always kept clean and dry? Is there enough room to get changed in comfort, and are there secure and large enough lockers? What is the standard of the showers and toilets? Look out for little touches, such as complimentary shampoo, plenty of mirrors and wall-mounted hair dryers.

* What is the timetable for the classes? Is it flexible and convenient enough for you?

* Will they give you a free day-pass to use the gym's facilities? Most reputable gyms should allow you to do this.

* Have you explained your real aims and ambitions to the instructor showing you around? Are you looking to lose weight, get fit, tone up, meet new people or all of these? Different gyms attract different personalities: have you found the right one for you? Is the club packed full of muscle boys or people looking to shed a few pounds? Is the gender and age balance right for you?

signing up

Once you have completed the grand tour, it's time to talk money. You will probably already have gauged what the monthly cost of being a member is, but you need to establish several more details. Begin by asking exactly what this fee includes. Does it cover all the services and classes, or are things such as yoga lessons and personal trainers going to cost more? Do you get a fresh towel each time you go, or will that cost extra?

Make sure you ask about the last price increase and whether another is planned in the near future. And when it comes to discussing the one-off joining fee, remember that many clubs give their sales staff flexibility in order to secure your signature. You will want to find out, too, what the terms are if you have to leave the gym. Are you entitled (as you should be) to a pro-rata rebate on your joining fee?

It's best to take any contract home before signing it, and to go through it carefully to see what would happen in the event of your

personal trainers

Finding the right trainer to monitor and motivate you can be the difference between reaching for the next dumb-bell weight, or reaching for the pizza delivery number. Whether you're assessing a trainer at the gym or a freelance local personal trainer, the line of questioning remains the same: are you compatible? In both cases, personal recommendations are best, but if you are looking for a freelance trainer, try looking in the local paper – or you could even ask your GP for advice.

When it comes to choosing, your first question should always be about their training and background. Again, you want trainers who are on the FIA's Register of Exercise Professionals. Another thing to look out for is whether they are part of the government's Exercise Referral Scheme. These are trainers that health professionals see fit to send people to if they have been recommended to exercise more.

A good trainer will give you a free consultation. They will also want to see whether you are compatible, and a good sign of this is if they ask you lots of questions as well as being a good listener. Ask to see their client references too.

In addition, ask them the following questions:

* When are you available?
* How many clients do you have on your books?
* What's your policy if I ever have to cancel at short notice?
* Do you charge an hourly fee or according to the service?
* Do you have personal liability insurance and first aid training?
* Why did you become a personal trainer, and do you keep up with the latest research and developments in your field?
* Would you be willing to share your time if I were to bring a friend or partner?

Keep thinking about compatibility. Will this trainer motivate you, and will you respond to their orders when the going gets tough? One last point to consider is whether you are happy with their gender. Many people – and their partners – have an issue about training with the opposite sex. After all, it's going to get very hot and sweaty.

leaving, or if the gym were to go bust or move premises. Distrust a gym that is reluctant to let you take away a contract to look over, and distrust it even more if it is determined to secure your signature on your first visit. Watch out, too, for new gyms that are still under construction offering special discounts 'only if you sign up today'. Once they're open, it is more than likely that they will continue with similar incentive schemes. The last thing you want to do is join a gym after an inspection that consists largely of dodging builders. And avoid 'life memberships' – are you really never going to move or at least want to move gyms?

With some of the gyms that belong to a chain or nationwide network, you should ask whether you can use the services of its sister branches with your membership for free, or at least a reduced fee. If you travel a lot, this is obviously a big advantage.

PRIMARY RESOURCES

FITNESS MAGAZINES

Health and Fitness
tel: 020 7331 1000
www.hfonline.co.uk

Men's Health
tel: 01858 438851
www.menshealth.co.uk

FITNESS ADVICE SITES

www.bbc.co.uk/health/fitness
www.thefitclub.com

FITNESS CLUB DIRECTORIES

www.abouthealthclubs.co.uk
www.clubhealth.co.uk
www.emotivate.co.uk
www.getsweaty.co.uk
www.gymuser.co.uk
www.health-club.net
www.thefitnessjungle.com

POPULAR FITNESS CLUBS

Cannons
tel: 08707 582146
www.cannons.co.uk

Courtneys
tel: 020 7792 2919
www.courtneys.co.uk

Curzons
tel: 020 7240 8411
www.curzons.com

David Lloyd
tel: 0870 888 3015
www.davidlloydleisure.co.uk

Esporta
tel: 0118 912 3500
www.esporta.co.uk

Fitness First
tel: 01202 845000
www.fitnessfirst.co.uk

Holmes Place
tel: 020 7795 4100
www.holmesplace.co.uk

LA Fitness
tel: 020 7366 8020
www.lafitness.co.uk

FITNESS CONSUMER SHOWS

Active at ExCeL, London
tel: 01483 870300
www.activeshow.co.uk

TRADE ASSOCIATIONS

Fitness Industry Association
tel: 020 7298 6730
www.fia.org.uk

The International Health, Racquet & Sportsclub Association
tel: 001 617 951 0055
www.ihrsa.org

The Sports Industries Federation
tel: 08708 709399
www.sportslife.org.uk

household electronics

the basics

The home entertainment market is undergoing huge change – or so retailers keep telling us. And guess what? You're meant to be keeping up with all those techno upgrades by buying all the latest electronic consumables, or 'brown goods' as the industry snappily calls them.

Just as we were persuaded to rush out to buy eight-track cartridges, Betamax videos and laserdiscs, we are now confronted with the Big Digital Quandary. Digital's victory over analogue is almost nigh, we are persistently told, so when are you going to jump aboard?

For the most part we already have, as shown by the dominance of CD players and our increasing love affair with digital satellite television services, but over the next few years it is expected that we will complete the transition by adopting DVD recorders instead of VCRs, digital radio sets instead of the wireless, and finally, all move over to digital television sets. Such is the leap in quality that it is hard to see analogue equipment surviving much more than a decade, especially as the industry (and government) makes it ever harder for us to stubbornly cling on to the old analogue world order by reducing our format options (have you tried to buy a new album on vinyl recently?) and, ultimately, by switching off the analogue TV signal (scheduled for between 2006 and 2010).

The staggering success of DVD over the last year suggests that we are not exactly being dragged kicking and screaming towards the digital age, but if you are planning on buying any brown goods, it is becoming more important to think about how well it will integrate with the rest of your equipment at home and, more importantly perhaps, with any future purchases. So as it becomes ever easier and more rewarding to hook up all your equipment together to create one singing and dancing entertainment beast, always be on the lookout for compatibility and connection capacity.

As staying in is apparently the new going out, you can start your purchasing cycle by settling down with some boys' toys mags and logging on to some review websites (see 'primary resources') to see what the market has to offer. Mugging up on the lingo is always key with electronic equipment, but what you should really be looking for is models that are one or two notches down from the latest release. Leave the white-hot, cutting-edge kit (and its high prices) to others.

audio equipment

Your hi-fi could, and should, be mission control for any entertainment system. If you buy yourself a decent amplifier and set of speakers, they will not only give your hi-fi system a solid foundation, but also make your meagre TV seem as though it's taken Viagra.

To perform this alchemy, you should be thinking about buying your hi-fi as different units, called 'separates' by the trade, rather than as a mini-tower. Popular hi-fi separates include an amplifier and speakers (essential), a radio tuner (sometimes combined with the amp), a CD player, a cassette deck and a turntable. These separates will give you much better quality for your money and will provide better future-proofing, as they can be chopped and changed at a whim without making the rest of the system redundant. There are a few drawbacks to separates, though, such as the increased tangle of cables behind the system and the prospect of extra remote controls to add to your vast collection, but these are small when compared to the advantages.

When you head down to the shops to try out a few models, take along one of your favourite CDs so that you can judge the equipment with something you are familiar with. You may find your CD a little easier on the ear, too, than the sales assistant's *Hardcore – You Know the Score* compilation album. And look for shops that have a listening room that ideally has been designed to simulate the acoustics of the average sitting room, namely, one with carpets, curtains and a three-piece suite.

Watch out, though, that you aren't trying out equipment plugged into a much higher quality amp and speakers, as it won't be a very fair comparison. You need to test like for like, so tell the assistant what you already have at home. If you're starting from scratch, choose the amp and speakers first.

It is also important to get high-quality cables. The system will only be as good as its weakest link, and you don't want to bring the system down with cheap cables. Good cable costs at least £5 a metre, and don't forget to get decent connectors too.

One last thing to think about when buying an amplifier is whether it has enough input sockets at the back. Most manufacturers build amps with at least four inputs nowadays, but if you want to connect your TV, DVD player and satellite box to the amp, you must find one that has enough capacity. While you are checking with the sales assistant, also ask them whether the amp will support 'surround sound' or 5.1 channel sound. This is what you need if you want to take full advantage of a DVD player or Nicam video player. It means the amp is capable of supporting left, centre and right speakers in addition to rear left, rear right and subwoofer speakers. In other words, you'll be listening to an orchestra rather than a school recital.

televisions

The Big Digital Quandary probably affects the buying of televisions more than anything else at the moment. For several years, the advice has been to rent your television and wait until the new digital sets become commonplace. There is a certain logic in this, but given that most televisions have an average life-span of about ten years and that the analogue switch-off is still a good five to ten years off, you aren't really going to be caught short – yet. And given that cheap digital set-top boxes are now available, buying a high-quality analogue TV can still make sense.

Do not head off to the shops, however, without working out what size you need. Measure the space available and how far away you will sit from the set to determine the correct size. Television sizes are determined according to the screen's diagonal width. A good guide is to sit no less than about twice as far from the screen as the screen measures diagonally. You also need at least an inch of room at the back for ventilation.

Just as with buying a hi-fi, it's a good idea to test a television in a specially designed room. Trying to judge the quality of a television in a busy shop with bright strip lighting and a bank of sets before you is far from ideal. What's more, you want to watch out for retailers who feed all those sets from a single – and thus weakened – aerial signal. A good retailer should have a special viewing room, but don't be won over if the sales staff show off the set with a DVD – it's hardly a fair comparison unless you have such facilities. Try and tune the sets yourself and change the colour, brightness and contrast to see the set's full range. And don't be won over by claims of exceptional resolution. Your eye is unlikely to be able to tell the difference between 600 and 800 lines of resolution, for example, so save your money.

When you're fiddling around with the set, use its remote control rather than the buttons of the set itself. You will rarely be using the set's controls, and you want to see if the remote has a sensible layout, as some have their buttons too close (a crucial detail for any dad or boyfriend). Check to see if the television's on-screen menu is intuitive to use, as many seem to be designed with a teenage boy's skilful fingers solely in mind.

Lastly, avoid those TV/video combo sets. Unless it is for a kitchen or bedroom, these seemingly handy sets can cause endless technical problems and are not really suited to the needs of the average sitting room. On the other hand, widescreen sets (16:9 scale screens rather than the more conventional 4:3 scale) are getting ever cheaper after some scarily high launch prices a few years back. More and more programmes and films are being made to match this format, and its future seems secure (which is not something you'll hear a lot of with brown goods).

DVD

There seems to be little doubt now that DVD has successfully won us over and escaped the tag of being just another format that failed to knock VHS off its perch, such as Laserdisc and Betamax before it. There was a huge leap in sales of DVDs in 2001, and many in the industry believe that the phenomenal sales of the animated blockbuster *Shrek* were the principal catalyst. What everyone is asking now is whether DVD recorders can penetrate the market to the same extent. They are presently quite rare and extremely expensive, but it seems inevitable that over the next few years they will become as common as VCRs today.

If you are thinking of joining the DVD revolution, you must make sure your television is up to scratch. There's little point in having a DVD player if you have anything less than a 27 in. television, and you should really, as stated earlier, be hooking it up to a decent hi-fi too.

When you are testing DVD players, try and get the sales staff to show you a pacy scene from a film such as *The Matrix*. You want to see how good the player is at handling fast, complex imagery and sounds. There's no point testing it on something like *Teletubbies*, with its slow, primary-coloured images.

You will hear a lot about having your DVD player 'chipped' when you are researching and testing different models. DVD players are configured to accept discs from certain regions around the world (the US is Region 1, Europe is Region 2 and so on). This allows the industry to meet local content and classification demands, as well as allowing for staggered global releases, as with movies. Cynics also suggest the industry is keeping a tight control on local markets and preventing illegal duplication – something it failed to do with the release of CDs.

Today's DVD players are currently quite easy to 'chip', namely be altered to let them play discs from different regions – some shops may even offer to do it for a fee. (It often just involves the keying-in of a short sequence of numbers on the remote.) It is very popular in the UK, because DVDs are relatively expensive here and can be bought much cheaper online from the US or the Far East. The industry is introducing new guards against chipping, such as RCE encoding, but it still isn't illegal to chip your machine. It will, however, invalidate the manufacturer's warranty.

For advice on how to chip the leading models and news about the industry's attempts to stop it, visit **www.dvd.reviewer.co.uk**.

VCRs

It may appear that the VCR's days are numbered given the assault of DVD, but video recorders are destined to be around for a good few years yet. And as a quality Nicam video can now cost as little as £130, they're better value than ever.

When shopping for one, ask if you can test the recording quality by using a blank tape. Most good shops should allow you to do this. When you are playing the recording back, test the pause button and fast-forward mechanisms. Does it perform these operations smoothly and without losing picture quality?

You should probably ignore, however, developments such as D-VHS (digital VHS), which is an attempt to update the quality of VHS to match DVD, but with little success. With DVD firmly on the scene, it is unlikely to catch on, so you will be wasting your money.

making your purchase

Buying brown goods can be quite intimidating. It invariably involves going head-to-head with a cocky young salesman who throws all the latest jargon at you and is convinced that a particular model is totally right for you. As ever, keep things under control by browsing through online reviews and the specialist magazines first so that you know what you want before you enter a store. By checking out some price-comparison sites and reputable online retailers (see 'primary resources'), you may even find a great bargain, but don't forget about delivery charges and import duties if buying from a site based outside the UK.

Don't ever be tempted by the 'bait and switch' deals that are common with brown goods retailers. This is when you see or hear an advert claiming the earth, only to find that the particular model advertised is now sold out or the offer has changed. The important thing for the retailer is that you are now in their shops and thus potential prey.

Similarly, be sceptical of price promises and low-price guarantees. While some shops will offer to match, or even beat the price of competitors (something that you should always exploit), the deals are just meaningless words in most cases.

Look out for end-of-line deals and seasonal sales when retailers are looking to make room for new stock, but ignore retailers who say they will beat the manufacturer's recommended retail price. There is no such thing with electronic goods, and in most cases, with mark-ups so low in such a competitive sector, retailers look to exploit the dreaded extended warranty as the best way to line their pockets.

ethics watch

When *Ethical Consumer* magazine last looked at TVs and videos, it found the working conditions to be the main issue of concern. Many of the predominantly Far Eastern conglomerates used 'export processing zone' factories in Mexico, where thousands of workers live in poverty. The area has also been described as having 'the highest levels of toxic exposure ever found in the world'. The magazine wrote to all the companies and asked them about their labour codes of conduct. Not one chose to offer safeguards.

One TV manufacturer, the Japanese conglomerate Mitsubishi, has also attracted worldwide notoriety regarding logging, and has interests in nuclear power and defence.

Taking into account the records of the producers on a range of social, environmental and animal welfare issues, *Ethical Consumer* recommended Grundig, followed by Bang & Olufsen and Casio.

When it last investigated DVD player manufacturers, the main issue of concern was the disposal of old equipment. New, 'improved' technologies have significant environmental costs, particularly when consumers are persuaded to discard 'old technology' before the end of its natural life. Electronic equipment is one of the largest known sources of heavy metals, toxic materials and organic pollutants in municipal waste.

Many of the producers of DVD players also make electronics for the defence industry. Sony, for example, makes video and audio equipment for the military, while Samsung is part of a group that makes fighter aircraft.

Taking into account the records of the producers on a range of social, environmental and animal welfare issues, the magazine's overall Best Buy advice for DVD player manufacturers was to choose Pioneer, Bush or Kenwood.

For more information, visit www.ethicalconsumer.org or call 0161 226 2929.

Retailers admit they stand to make between 40 and 65 per cent on selling extended warranties to consumers. If brown goods fail, the statistics show that it will tend to happen either in the first few weeks or towards the end of its natural life – a trend known as the 'bathtub curve'. As manufacturers guarantee most goods for a year anyway (often doubled by a credit card firm if you buy through them), is it really worth buying an expensive extended warranty?

One last thought on comparison shopping: remember that manufacturers often make special models uniquely for the larger nationwide retailers. For this reason, always note down the exact model number and key features when comparing what seem to be similar items. And when browsing comparison-shopping websites, remember that many of them are affiliated to a limited range of online retailers, so you may not exactly be getting an accurate picture of what prices are available.

Oh, and always ask for a discount. You'll be surprised how many shops are open to offers – it's not just for the hagglers of London's Tottenham Court Road.

expert view

Ian Calcutt, editor of *Home Entertainment*, offers the following useful tips:

Don't be persuaded to spend money on lots of new features, as it's unlikely you will use them all. However, TVs bursting with rear sockets are recommended. Who knows what you might want to connect them to in the future?

A good tip is to look for an integrated audio-visual receiver that includes a radio tuner, stereo amplification for CDs and surround sound for movies. This should serve most of your audio needs.

To get the most out of DVD digital soundtracks, use an AV amplifier or receiver with Dolby Digital and DTS compatibility. You will, however, need extra speakers and cables.

Choose your optimum screen size carefully, as films and most new TV shows are widescreen. Integrated digital sets aren't essential, however, as you can just add an adaptor box later.

Above 32 in., standard TVs get bulky, but large plasma or LCD screens can go on or against a wall. They do, however, come at a price. Rear-projection sets aren't ideal in bright environments, while stand-alone projectors require a screen and blacked-out room but are perfect for true 'home cinema'.

Tired of videotape? Recordable DVD is still expensive, and comes in competing formats, but cost-effective hard-drive video devices like TiVo and Sky+ are excellent at time-shifting (and then disposing of) programmes. Hybrids combining hard drives with VHS or DVD are also appearing.

Remember that TV or video equipment bought overseas may not be compatible with UK broadcasts.

PRIMARY RESOURCES

LEADING MANUFACTURERS

Aiwa
tel: 0870 168 9000
www.aiwa.co.uk

Akai
tel: 0113 251 1500
www.akai.com

Alba (includes Bush and Goodmans)
tel: 020 8594 5533

Bang & Olufsen
tel: 01189 692288
www.bang-olufsen.co.uk

Bose
tel: 0870 741 4500
www.bose.com

Casio
tel: 020 8208 9450
www.casio.co.uk

Denon
tel: 01234 741200
www.denon.com

Grundig
tel: 020 8324 9400
www.grundig.co.uk

Hitachi
tel: 0345 581455
www.hitachi.co.uk

JVC
tel: 0870 168 9000
www.jvc.co.uk

Kenwood
tel: 01923 816444
www.kenwood-electronics.co.uk

LG
tel: 0870 607 5544
www.lgelectronics.co.uk

Mitsubishi
tel: 001 949 465 6000
www.mitsubishi-tv.com

NAD
tel: 01296 482017
www.nad.co.uk

Panasonic
tel: 08705 357357
www.panasonic.co.uk

Philips
tel: 020 8665 6350
www.philips.co.uk

Pioneer
tel: 01753 789789
www.pioneer.co.uk

Samsung
tel: 020 8391 0168
www.samsungelectronics.co.uk

Sanyo
tel: 01923 246363
www.sanyo.co.uk

Sharp
tel: 0800 262958
www.sharp.co.uk

Sony
tel: 08705 111999
www.sony.co.uk

TEAC
tel: 01923 819630
www.teac.co.uk

Technics
tel: 08705 357357
www.technics.co.uk

Thomson
tel: 01732 520920
www.thomson-europe.com

Toshiba
tel: 01932 828828
www.toshiba.co.uk

Yamaha
tel: 01923 233166
www.yamaha-audio.co.uk

HIGH-STREET RETAILERS

Comet
tel: 0845 600 7002
www.comet.co.uk

Currys
tel: 0500 304304
www.currys.co.uk

Dixons
tel: 0800 682868
www.dixons.co.uk

John Lewis
tel: 020 7629 7711
www.johnlewis.com

Richer Sounds
tel: 0870 011 2345
www.richersounds.com

ONLINE RETAILERS

www.amazon.co.uk
www.appliance-direct.co.uk
www.bedirect.co.uk
www.discount-electrical-goods.co.uk
www.electricaldiscountuk.co.uk
www.empiredirect.co.uk
www.hifibitz.co.uk
www.jungle.com
www.qed-uk.com
www.techtronics.com/uk/shop
www.unbeatable.co.uk
www.value-direct.co.uk
www.webelectricals.co.uk

PRICE-COMPARISON WEBSITES

www.dealtime.co.uk
http://uk.kelkoo.com
www.uk.pricerunner.com
http://uk.shopping.yahoo.com/home
_entertainment
http://uk.shopsmart.com

REVIEW WEBSITES

www.cnet.com
www.consumerreview.com
www.consumer-reviews.co.uk
www.deja.com
www.dooyoo.co.uk
www.ecoustics.com/home/
www.epinions.com
www.reviewfinder.com
www.uk.ciao.com

MAGAZINES

Hi-Fi Choice
tel: 01458 271147
www.hifichoice.co.uk

Home Entertainment
tel: 01458 271171
www.home-entertainment.co.uk

T3
tel: 01458 271100
www.t3.co.uk

Total DVD
tel: 020 7331 1000
www.totaldvd.net

What Video & TV
tel: 020 7331 1000
www.whatvideotv.com

TRADE ASSOCIATIONS

Association of Manufacturers of Domestic Electrical Appliances
tel: 020 7405 0666

Domestic Appliance Service Association
tel: 01920 872464
www.dasa.org.uk

Radio, Electrical and Television Retailers' Association
tel: 01234 269110
www.retra.co.uk

kitchens and bathrooms

the basics

'The bathroom and kitchen will need some updating.' If you ever hear this combination of words fall from an estate agent's lips, it can mean only two things. First, brace yourself, as you're about to be shown an avocado-green bathroom suite and kitchen bedecked with cork-effect linoleum flooring. Second, forget about buying that new designer sofa for your new sitting room, because the money you've been saving up is needed elsewhere.

Getting a new kitchen or bathroom is still considered one of the best investments you can make in your home. Many estate agents even believe that money spent wisely on these two key rooms will easily be recouped when you come to sell. But investing time and money in a new kitchen and bathroom isn't just about getting that fantasy room you've seen while flicking through the glossy interiors magazines: it's also about wrestling with an industry that has, let us say, a less than savoury reputation.

Pick up a newspaper or watch any consumer programme and it won't take long before you hear a tale of a kitchen or bathroom company that has walked off with clients' deposits, left jobs incomplete, performed shoddy work, or, worse, gone bankrupt. Doing up these rooms is not something that should be done on a whim: ideally, it is something that you should have researched for weeks, if not months, before you even entertain the idea of handing over any money.

Your first task on the road to power showers and stainless-steel splashbacks is to make a list of what you currently hate about your rooms and what you would ideally like from the end result. Add to this list practicalities such as where and what your energy sources are; whether you are likely to need any structural work done like moving walls; and where your current soil pipes and waste drainage outlets are. You will soon start to get an idea of which of your design dreams are practical. More importantly, perhaps, you will soon gauge whether the job is going to involve taking out a loan equal in size to a small country's national debt.

Once you have a good idea of what you want, you can set about working out how this fantasy is going to be turned into reality. You only have three realistic options: do it yourself (with or without the help of a builder); use the services of a DIY supermarket; or use the services of a specialist fitting company.

Your decision will largely be determined by whether your DIY skills are up to the job, which, in reality, is unlikely. Fitting bathrooms and kitchens isn't like papering the spare room over a weekend – it invariably requires the handiwork of professionals. It may even require planning permission (always check with your local council before starting any major work). And out of all the botched DIY jobs that you could ever do, a bad kitchen or bathroom has got to be the most detrimental to the look and value of your home. This really is a case of getting what you pay for. Cutting corners and quick fixes should not be on your agenda.

If you do want to call in the pros, you can begin by shooing away any cold callers or doorsteppers. You want to research and then approach your target candidates on your terms, so also avoid the temptation of being lured by all those 'special offers' that 'include a free dishwasher' or 'must end this week' especially beloved by the specialist fitters.

You're looking for specialists who ask lots of questions about your requirements, and understand your habits and needs. They should show you their selection of products and services in a dedicated showroom, rather than by flicking through a brochure on your sofa. Be suspicious if they start getting itchy for you to sign contracts and part with a deposit before you are ready. Ideally, you will need at least three detailed quotes with a breakdown of costs, a timetable of works and payments, and a full explanation of cancellation costs and after-sales guarantees. When it does come to crunch time, the deposit should be about a quarter of the total cost, and if it is over £100 (it will be, don't worry), you should aim to pay for it on a credit card, as the payment protection the card companies offer will help guard against bankruptcies and rogue traders.

Lastly, avoid any of those finance packages they may dangle enticingly before you. You'll inevitably get much better rates by shopping around for loans yourself. And don't sign any satisfaction agreements before you are 100 per cent sure the job has been done to your satisfaction rather than theirs, as it's not uncommon for companies to try and rush you into signing on the dotted line before you have made your last payment or before the job is properly finished.

kitchens

It's unlikely you will spend more on anything else in your home other than, perhaps, a new roof or extension. It's an understandable expenditure, too, considering that some of us spend up to 40 per cent of our entire time in the kitchen and have even turned them into the principal family room in some cases. We spend over £600 million a year on fitted kitchens, and half of those are bought through a DIY supermarket.

If you are going for specialist help, begin the search by limiting yourself to members of well-known trade associations, such as the Kitchen Specialists Association (KSA), or firms that can boast the Furniture Industry Research Association (FIRA) Gold Award. Contact both associations for the members nearest to you. This will immediately give you the peace of mind that the firm you are dealing with is being vigorously vetted. KSA members should also have signed up to the Qualitas furnishing standards and to KSA ConsumerCare, which is an insurance scheme to protect against unfinished work and withheld deposits. Insist on all these points if they are a KSA member and wait to see if they ask you questions such as these:

* Do you intend to keep pets in the kitchen?
* Do you want your appliances hidden?
* How many pots and pans do you have?
* Do you need lots of storage for dried goods?
* What type of boiler do you have?

In other words, they should be thinking hard about the ergonomics and usability of the kitchens, and you should be left to concentrate on things like the colour of the doors or the shape of the handles. Fitted kitchens can now, with the aid of computers, be designed to fit into and make the best use of the smallest of kitchens, so expect your kitchen designer to fully exploit the space you have.

When you go round the showrooms looking at the products available, pay particular attention to the quality of the materials used. The 'carcass' of nearly every kitchen unit made today is made of chipboard. This isn't necessarily bad, but you should make sure it is completely covered with a laminated surface to prevent water penetration. Save your money for better quality doors, drawers and fascias, rather than forking out more to upgrade from a chipboard carcass. You may also want to enquire if you can save money by reusing the carcass you already have and just pay for new doors and worktops. In most cases, they will be fine to be reused and you may just have to buy a few extra units (the standard double unit size is 1,000 mm wide × 600 mm deep × 900 mm high) depending on the design. Remember, too, that units that may appear to be made by different companies because of their brand name are often made by the same company, so shop around looking for telltale similarities.

One area that seems to regularly irritate people is the quality of drawer runners. You should be looking for a minimum of three rollers on each side of the drawers to help keep them stable and moving smoothly. And make sure the units have adjustable feet, so that they can be moulded to fit a wobbly floor, and that the wall brackets are metal, rather than plastic, for extra strength.

The biggest choice available to you will probably be which material you use for your worktop. Formica (plastic-laminated wood) has been the popular choice for decades now, but recent years have seen the rise of stainless steel, quality woods and even granite. All have their pros and cons (and expense) depending on your needs, but this is one part of the kitchen that you want to be fitted with particular care and skill, as it is one of the most visible. If you are planning on fitting it yourself, ask for Pro-Joint systems, which will help you keep the job looking professional.

When it comes to appliances (and even sinks), it is best to shop around for bargains, particularly online. There should be no obligation to use those offered by the company fitting the kitchen. Many firms will have a very limited range, and even push preferred brands. Most units and appliances are now made to standard sizes (600 mm × 600 mm × 900 mm high, in most cases), and it should be easy to slot in an appliance after the kitchen units have been fitted, as long as all the plumbing and electrics are correctly in place and the fitters are aware of what's coming. Don't be bullied into buying their appliances and don't forget that you can buy reconditioned appliances – particularly useful if you're planning on installing an expensive Aga.

bathrooms

Things get a bit simpler when it comes to bathrooms. They are generally easier to install yourself compared to kitchens, although it is highly recommended that you employ a plumber to do any fiddly pipe and drainage work. But the same rule still applies: if you are employing a specialist fitter, stick to ones that are members of trade associations such as the Bathroom Association.

You will undoubtedly save money by buying a bathroom suite in one go rather than buying items separately. And try to stick to the basic classic white suites if you are likely to sell your home in the near to medium future, as there have been too many crimes of bad taste committed in this area for anything other than white to be your choice. Express your own personality with details like styled taps, mirrors and radiators. Likewise, think plain and classic when it comes to the style and colour of any tile work you have. It will always be a positive influence on your home's saleability.

Other than style decisions, you are advised to think carefully about some of the safety and practical issues. If you have a steel or cast-iron bath it must be BSI-approved and earthed; mirrors should be well lit; there should be good ventilation; and lights and electrical appliances should be out of hand's reach.

Lastly, if possible, try to install a quality shower (particularly if you live in the Southeast, where estate agents claim that power showers are near-necessities these days). You must, however, consider your boiler's oomph. Combi boilers, for example, require mixer systems and can't be plumbed to a power shower's special electric pump.

from specialist fitters

You have two options: go for one of the big household names such as Magnet and Moben, or go for a local specialist. Whoever you choose, go for those that are trade association members (ring the association to be sure), and better still, those that have been recommended to you by a trusted friend or relative. Expand the safety net by checking with your local trading standards office to see if the firm has any reported problems. The general reputation, perceived or otherwise, of this sector is so bad that you can never do enough research on your shortlisted firms.

Visit their showrooms, tell them what you are after and book a time for them to come round for a 'site survey'. When they come to present you with a quote, make sure that it isn't just a 'guide price' – you want a detailed breakdown of the job in writing, as well as how long it will take and exactly what the terms and conditions entail.

If you proceed with the job, start keeping a daily log – of the workers' timekeeping (or lack of it), the progress and standard of the work – and take regular photographs as proof. It could all prove invaluable should you ever end up in a dispute with the firm.

from DIY stores

Most of the big DIY chains such as Homebase, Do It All, Wickes and B&Q offer an in-house fitting service, as well as the products required to fit out a kitchen or bathroom. This may be the cheapest fitting option available to you, but remember that most of them simply sub-contract out the work to a local fitter who may, or may not, be a member of a trade association. You will, in essence, be paying that DIY chain a fee to find that fitter for you. Could you have found them, or someone better, yourself?

It's also worth remembering when you're shopping around for quotes that some of the DIY chains are part of the same parent group. Focus Do It All, for example, owns and operates Focus, Great Mills, Do It All and Wickes.

be your own foreman

A daunting option for many, but organizing the job yourself could save you money. Your main investment, however, other than the final cost, is time. Don't entertain this option lightly. Prepare for standing rows with builders, invasion of your personal space, noise and lots of mess.

When you start looking for builders, plumbers and electricians, again, the advice is always to stick to members of trade associations. Contact the National Federation of Builders (NFB) and the Institute of Plumbers for advice and local contacts, and, if possible, spend £9.95 on one of the NFB's ready-made contracts that let you and the builder sign up in writing to crucial things like who makes the tea and what the toilet arrangements should be (this isn't a joke, by the way). If you want the job done by a certain date (who doesn't?), write that date with 'time is of the essence' next to it. And if you are going to need planning permission for anything – moving supporting walls, for example – determine who is responsible for organizing this (you, in most cases).

Additional checks should be made about whether the builder is VAT-registered (beware the VAT-free deal), and whether the plumber is CORGI-registered if they are going to be dealing with gas or boilers.

Your own builder can be handy for securing some trade prices. Get them to take you to the nearest 'trade-only' wholesalers and go shopping with them. Kitchen units, for example, are much cheaper this way. After all, most of the local special fitters will be buying their stock from such places, too.

Another good idea is to visit as many trade shows as possible. Some will be trade-only, but if you can build a good relationship with your builder, he might be willing to take you along. They are great for inspiration and ideas too, when you feel like all those showrooms are beginning to blur into one.

Don't proceed with any builder, however, without getting adequate insurance for the period of the job. For advice, contact the NFB. It has its own scheme, called the Benchmark Plan, but many insurance brokers will cover building work, so shop around.

---

expert view

Caroline Murphy, editor of *Kitchens, Bedrooms & Bathrooms* magazine, gives her need-to-know advice:

* To help illustrate your ideas, show the designer magazine clippings and brochures. This will help narrow down your colour, material and style preferences.

* Choose a company that will professionally measure and survey the space where your new kitchen or bathroom will be installed. After all, you don't want to be the one accountable should the specially ordered fridge-freezer or shower tray not fit its designated space.

* Read the small print carefully and be sure that all responsibilities are clarified. Who will be in charge of ripping out and disposing of the old kitchen or bathroom? Who will be responsible for decoration of floors, walls and ceilings? And for lighting, other electrics or plumbing? And what works must be completed before the new kitchen or bathroom arrives?

* Make sure the agreed schedule of payments is in writing. The final sum should be retained until the kitchen or bathroom is delivered and you are fully satisfied with it.

* When you're taking delivery of goods, open the boxes and check the products before you sign to say the items were delivered in satisfactory condition. If the courier won't wait, amend the delivery note to say 'Goods Unseen' before you sign.

* Find out what your water pressure is before you buy your bathroom brassware or kitchen taps. The majority of UK homes have low water pressure (less than 0.1 bar), whereas most Continental-made brassware is suited only to high-pressure systems. A pump or combi boiler can increase your water flow if you're determined to have the latest slick German or Italian styling.

PRIMARY RESOURCES

DIY ADVICE SITES

www.buildadvice.com
www.buildituk.com
www.diy.com (click on 'DIY advice')

LOCAL SPECIALIST SEARCH SITES

www.kitchenbuyersguide.com
www.plumblink.com
www.scoot.co.uk
www.yell.com

DIY CHAINS

B&Q
tel: 0845 309 3099
www.diy.com

Focus Do It All
tel: 0800 436436
www.focusdoitall.co.uk

IKEA
tel: 020 8208 5600
www.ikea.co.uk

Jewson
tel: 0800 539766
www.jewson.co.uk

MFI
tel: 0870 609 5555
www.mfi.co.uk

Travis Perkins
tel: 01604 752424
www.travisperkins.co.uk

Wickes
tel: 0500 300328
www.wickes.co.uk

BATHROOM RETAILERS

Armitage Shanks
tel: 01543 490253
www.armitage-shanks.co.uk

Aston Matthews
tel: 020 7226 7220
www.astonmatthews.co.uk

Bathroom Discount
tel: 020 7381 4222
www.bathroomdiscount.co.uk

Bathroom Warehouse
tel: 01491 832321
www.ukbw.co.uk

Bathstore.com
tel: 07000 228478
www.bathstore.com

Dolphin
tel: 0800 626717
www.dolphinbathrooms.com

Ideal Standard
tel: 01482 346461
www.ideal-standard.co.uk

Twyford
tel: 01270 879777
www.twyfordbathrooms.com

KITCHEN RETAILERS

Kitchens Direct
tel: 020 8342 1780
www.kitchendirect.co.uk

Magnet
tel: 01482 825451
www.magnet.co.uk

Manhattan Furniture
tel: 01903 524300
www.manhattan.co.uk

Moben
tel: 0800 413413
www.moben.co.uk

New Kitchen DIY
tel: 01780 766651
www.newkitchendiy.com

Smallbone
tel: 020 7581 9989
www.smallbone.co.uk

Symphony
tel: 0113 230 8000
www.symphony-group.co.uk

TRADE ASSOCIATIONS

Bathroom Association
  tel: 01782 747123
  www.bathroom-association.org

Council for Registered Gas
Installers (CORGI)
  tel: 01256 372200
  www.corgi-gas.com

Furniture Industry Research
Association (includes Qualitas)
  tel: 01438 777700
  www.fira.co.uk

Kitchen Specialists Association
  tel: 01905 726066
  www.ksa.co.uk

National Federation of Builders
  tel: 020 7608 5150
  www.builders.org.uk

National Home Improvements
Council
  tel: 020 7828 8230
  www.nhic.org.uk

TRADE SHOWS

Bathrooms and Kitchens Expo
(Held in May at ExCeL, London)
  tel: 020 8715 8307
  www.bkexpo.co.uk

BBC Good Homes (held in May at
Birmingham NEC)
  tel: 0870 264 5555
  www.bbcgoodhomesshow.co.uk

Homebuilding and Renovation
Show (held in March at
Birmingham NEC)
  tel: 020 7970 6518
  www.homebuildingshow.co.uk

Ideal Home Exhibition (held in
March at Earl's Court, London and
in October at the SECC, Glasgow)
  tel: 0870 606 6080
  www.idealhomeshow.co.uk

Interbuild (held in June at
Birmingham NEC)
  tel: 020 7505 6895
  www.interbuild.com

MAGAZINES

Bathrooms and Kitchens (trade)
  tel: 01858 438872
  www.bathroomskitchens.co.uk

Kitchens, Bedrooms & Bathrooms
  tel: 020 8515 2000
  www.dmg.co.uk/kbbmag

mobile phones

the basics

In an industry that boasts over forty million customers in the UK, you would think that a wide range of companies would be fighting one another to offer you scores of amazing deals – the perfect vision of a free market.

Sadly, the stark truth is that one of the most successful growth industries of the last decade is controlled by a handful of companies all fighting one another for your business by offering you near-impenetrable cost permutations and little in the way of unbiased advice. In short, buying a suitable mobile phone at a good price is one of the consumer's most challenging tests.

A fast-moving, cutting-edge industry unchecked by the discipline of credible regulation has led to a free-for-all. The only option for consumers is to roll up their sleeves and take on the mobile phone retailers on their own terms. Arm yourself with time, flexibility, knowledge and above all knowing how, when, why and where you plan to use a mobile phone.

You should therefore begin your quest by trying to establish your likely phone habits. What volume of calls do you plan to make each month? Will these calls be made at the weekend, evenings, during business hours, or an equal mix? Will they be to landlines or other mobile users? Are you a gossip, or are you quick and to the point on the phone? Do you want to use your phone abroad?

These are just some of the questions you need to answer before traipsing off down the high street. If you have trouble answering any of them, consider that, on average, people use their mobile phone for 42 minutes a month – 18 minutes during peak times and 23 minutes off-peak (weekends and evenings). And always ask as many mobile users as you can about their normal habits and costs.

the networks

Your first priority is to choose which network to use. There are only four companies that run and control their own 'network' of mobile phone infrastructure, namely O2 (formerly BT Cellnet), T-Mobile (formerly One 2 One), Orange and Vodafone. You also have the option of using a Virtual Network Operator (VNO), which leases lines by riding piggyback on one of the four main networks; VNOs currently include Virgin Mobile, Fresh! (both via T-Mobile) and Genie (via O2). Confusing matters still further, the four networks sell their services to customers through either their own-brand high-street shops or through affiliated retailers. The only truly independent retailer is the Carphone Warehouse, which sells services from all four networks, but also owns the Fresh! VNO. Got all that?

The largest and oldest of the networks are O2 and Vodafone. Both boast that they offer the best coverage, namely, the quality and reach of their services across the UK, but as reception can be affected by local obstacles such as hills or tall buildings, it is best to check each network's coverage by doing your own postcode search via their websites (see 'primary resources'). Alternatively, a retailer will give you a detailed answer.

It is also wise to check which networks your friends and family use. You will invariably be charged more to call rival networks, so you can keep your costs down by trying to make sure that as many as possible of the numbers you are likely to call belong to your network.

tariffs

The key decision to make when buying a mobile phone is choosing which network's tariff – pricing system – you will use. There are hundreds of options available to you, but don't fall into the trap of believing there are good and bad tariffs. There are simply suitable and unsuitable tariffs. What is good to a business user will clearly not suit someone who just wants a phone for emergencies. This is why it is important to have a good idea of your likely phone habits before you begin to compare tariffs.

Make sure you always establish what a network means by peak and off-peak calls (peak calls are usually 7am–7pm, Monday to Friday). And do you really need to pay more for extra services such as text messaging, voicemail (ansaphone), WAP, internet access or email? All this will help you determine which type of pay-as-you-go deal or monthly contract you opt to buy.

pay-as-you-go deals

This method is largely responsible for the huge explosion of popularity in mobiles over the last few years. Pay-as-you-go phones make an ideal gift, because the buyer pays one up-front price, then the user tops up their credit through vouchers. There is no need to commit to a 12-month contract, go through credit checks, pay connection and line rental charges, and have the headache of monthly bills. The handsets that come with pay-as-you-go deals were initially hugely subsidized, allowing buyers to pick up deals for just £30 or so, but the networks have cut back their subsidies over the last year and pay-as-you-go deals now start at around £60. Even so, pay-as-you-go is still preferred by a majority of low- to mid-level users due to its convenience and simplicity. However, the sting of pay-as-you-go usually comes in the form of higher call costs.

contract deals

The more conventional contract deals allow the networks to recoup the costs of subsidized handsets and cheaper call charges through your 12-month commitment to their line rental charges, typically between £15 and £30 a month. High-end users prefer contract deals because of the seemingly generous inclusive minutes available. That's to say, the minutes of free calls before you have to start paying by the minute. Most contract deals will give you hundreds of inclusive minutes free a month, but you must ask exactly what inclusive means. Are calls to mobiles on other networks or landlines included? At what time can these inclusive minutes be used? Can I carry over any unused inclusive minutes from month to month? Typically, the more you pay a month in line rental charges, the less your calls will cost beyond any inclusive allowance.

Again, you must ask for a precise breakdown of the call costs awaiting you beyond your inclusive allowance. Charges can fluctuate between anything from 2p a minute to landlines at weekends and 35p a minute to mobiles on different networks. When considering contract deal charges it always helps to think what your annual cost is likely to be rather than be attracted to the low sign-up deals.

extra services

* *text messaging:* The most popular mobile phone service beyond simply making calls. It was born when the networks switched from analogue to digital systems, and its success took the networks by surprise. After all, why would spending minutes keying in a message that would take seconds to say be popular? Because it's much cheaper, and like email, waits until its recipient is ready to receive it. It is also convenient if you don't want to engage in a full conversation. It comes as standard on all phones these days and usually costs between 5p and 12p to send each message. However, many monthly contract deals include a number of free text messages in their inclusive minutes.

* *voicemail:* Another standard feature on all mobile phones, but one that can be expensive. To listen to your messages can cost from a few pence a minute up to a frightening 40p a minute. Charges can vary depending on when you use the service. T-Mobile stands alone in offering free voicemail retrieval on all its tariffs.

* *itemized bills:* Even though networks can charge up to £3 a month for itemized bills, it is well worth the investment, if only to help you control and budget your costs. Orange and T-Mobile do not currently charge for itemized bills on any of their tariffs.

* *roaming:* The ability to use your phone abroad is becoming increasingly popular, but UK roamers are currently being charged twice by the networks, a move which has been criticized by the telecoms regulator, Oftel. Controversially, you are charged for

making a call and for receiving calls, so ask the networks for a detailed breakdown of their roaming charges. Check which type of handset – dual band or triband – you have too, as Europe and the US, for example, use different systems. It's worth checking for compatibility across the world on the GSM website (Global System for Mobile Communication, **www.gsmworld.com**).

If you are planning to roam frequently, you may be better off taking out your SIM card (Subscriber Identity Module, the removable microchip that holds your account and personal details) and hiring a local one for the duration of your visit. The networks are getting wise to this, though, and some 'lock' your phone. If they let you, they will typically charge about £35 to unlock it, but this could still prove to be a saving in the long run. You can check if a phone is locked by seeing if a SIM card from a different network works in it.

* *wap/email/3G:* The arrival of interactive services was greeted with great fanfare in 1999, but has, so far, failed to lived up to the networks' and public's expectations. The facility to access a very limited form of the internet and email via Wap-enabled (Wireless Application Protocol) phones failed to catch on, and now the industry awaits the launch of the much-heralded 3G – third-generation – phones, which promise to offer videophone facilities and near-full internet access. The networks have invested billions of pounds in securing 3G licences, so expect aggressive marketing and tempting deals when it finally launches. As with most new technologies, however, it may be best to hold back a few months and let the market settle down before taking the plunge.

NB: To compare and contrast the minutiae of all the networks' deals and tariffs, it is a good idea to get hold of a copy of *What Mobile* or *What Cellphone* magazine to see their up-to-date network comparison charts. If you try and glean all this information from sales people on the high street, you will just come away even more confused. You should also try some tariff-comparison websites (see 'primary resources').

And don't be afraid to swap tariffs if your lifestyle and phone habits change. You may have to buy your way out of a monthly contract, but it could be worth it if it means not being tied to an unsuitable tariff.

the phones

Your choice of handset should always be secondary to your choice of network and tariff, but there are some important features to look out for.

Practically speaking, battery performance is the phone's most important feature. You want to ask about the phone's standby time and talktime, namely, how long the phone can be on before the battery needs recharging and how long the battery lasts when you're constantly making calls. Standby times on new phones have increased dramatically in the last year. You should expect a phone to offer over 120 hours of standby and ideally four or more hours of talktime.

A popular new accessory is the emergency charger – a battery pack that you carry with you, allowing you to charge up your phone when away from a power point. They are undeniably convenient, but are a worrying move away from a recharging culture towards a disposable battery culture.

The appeal of the phone's appearance will, of course, be personal to you, but it's worth remembering that mobile snobs seem, for style reasons, to dislike Motorola phones, so dealers will often try to push their Motorola stock first. Likewise, the same mobile snobs took a dislike to BT Cellnet (now O2). If you enter a shop saying you're not too bothered about the names involved, that you just want a good deal, don't be surprised to be offered a Motorola phone running on O2. There isn't necessarily anything wrong with this, but don't be fobbed off.

Other features you will want to consider are the number of phone-book spaces available (which should be over a hundred), predictive text input when you're text messaging (it will save you developing a sore thumb), voice-activated dialling, the weight (anything under 100 grams is considered light) and the size (does it fit comfortably into a trouser pocket?).

If you have health concerns about the levels of radio-frequency

ethics watch

Mobile phone manufacturers use a rare mineral called coltan, because it is an excellent conductor that can be used to coat a phone's electronic components. The ore is nearly as heavy as gold and 80 per cent of the world's reserves are in Africa, with 80 per cent of those in Congo. Observers in Africa say the search for coltan is funding the war in Congo – Africa's biggest – and is, like the lucrative illegal diamond trade, even a root cause of the fighting.

Environmentalists believe that coltan mining is also a threat to wildlife, claiming that miners are disturbing gorillas and killing thousands of elephants for food. Nokia, Motorola and other mobile phone producers insist that their suppliers no longer use coltan from Congo, but make sure you always ask where a phone's coltan is sourced.

When *Ethical Consumer* magazine assessed mobile phones in October 1999, all of the top ten mobile phone brands in the UK had links with the arms industry. NEC and Samsung both produced missile guidance systems, Ericsson produced pulse radar for combat aircraft, and Nokia manufactured anti-aircraft systems and coastal artillery applications.

Siemens warranted a special mention, not only for building nuclear power stations, but also for its involvement in the controversial Narmarda dam project, which is displacing over two hundred thousand Indian peasant farmers in Gujarat.

Taking into account a whole range of social and environmental factors, One 2 One (now T-Mobile) was the *Ethical Consumer*'s best-buy network, while Bosch and Nokia were the best for phones.

The report also recommended looking out for one of the many charity recycling schemes for those who already have a mobile and wish to upgrade.

For more information, visit www.ethicalconsumer.org or call 0161 226 2929.

(RF) radiation emitted from your phone, ask what its SAR (Specific Absorption Rate) is. All phones in the UK easily meet the National Radiological Protection Board's limit of 10 watts per kilogram (w/kg), but some phone levels are now as low as 0.5 w/kg. The Federation of Electronic Industries insists that all new mobiles now list SAR levels, but as yet, there is no universally agreed standard for low SAR levels.

Lastly, it may be worth checking the version of software in your phone. Just like any new software release, the early versions can sometimes be unstable and buggy. For instance, one of 2001's best sellers, the Nokia 6210, was buggy until it was installed with Version 4 of its software. If a phone starts acting up, check which version of the software is installed by entering the manufacturer's release code. For example, on Nokia phones enter *#0000#.

insurance

Contrary to popular belief, household insurance rarely covers mobile phones against theft or loss. Only 30 per cent of mobiles in the UK are insured, which is surprising when you consider how expensive it can be to replace one. If you lose a contract phone, you are still committed to pay your twelve months of line rental, and you must replace the originally subsidized phone at cost price, which can amount to well over £100. So get insurance.

Most contract phone cover will cost between £3 and £6 a month, depending on your network and phone. Pay-as-you-go phone insurance varies hugely (anywhere between £12 and £50 a year), but remember that you can shop around. Always ask the following questions:

- Do I have to pay an excess fee?
- How do I make a claim?
- Am I covered for accidental damage?
- Will I automatically be given a replacement phone, or can I get a cash alternative?
- What happens if my phone is no longer available?

The main fear of having your phone stolen is that the thief will run up huge costs in unauthorized calls. One way you can limit this damage is to ask if you can have a credit limit placed on your phone. Once this limit is exceeded, the phone will be blocked.

You can help police make a crime report by keeping a record of your phone's unique ID, or IMEI, number. It can usually be found behind the battery, but you can also read it by keying *#06# into your phone.

Under extreme pressure from consumers and the government, the networks have now agreed to immediately block phones that have been reported stolen. This should dramatically cut the amount of mobile phone crime, but until it becomes universally introduced, it is worth getting as much protection as possible.

expert view: free!* free!* free!*

Perdita Patterson, editor of *What Mobile* magazine, urges you to be suspicious when retailers throw around the word 'free':

* *free mini TV!** If there's an asterisk by it, you'll usually find that the freebie only comes with the most expensive tariff the network has to offer. Or it may be that it has – alas – sold out now and you can have a £20 gift voucher instead. This will not be anything like the value of the promised gift. Most deals also come with standard accessories, so don't be impressed by the 'free' headset, car-lighter charger and swap-in fascia.

* *free £50 cashback!* Plenty of contract deals advertise cashback, sometimes as much as £100. The catch is that you don't get it back until you've spent considerably more than that and stayed with the contract tariff for a specified length of time, usually over a year. You'll probably have to apply for it, too. They call this redemption, and in many cases, it will only come in the form of credit on your bill.

* *free connection!* Come on – nearly everybody gives free connection. Big deal.

* *free two months' line rental!* You will register for this, respectively, six months after you sign and a year after you sign. Again, it will be in the form of redemption, so you have to pay for it first and apply for the rebate later.

* *free three months' insurance!* You will probably find that it is activated after a year of using the service.

* *free delivery when buying online!* Unless you want it to arrive on a Saturday, that is, and then it will cost you around £11.99.

* *five free ringtones and graphics!* Again, only by redemption.

PRIMARY RESOURCES

THE NETWORKS

O2 (formerly BT Cellnet)
tel: 0870 521 4000
www.o2.co.uk

Orange
tel: 0500 802080
www.orange.co.uk

T-Mobile (formerly One 2 One)
tel: 0808 121 3000
www.t-mobile.co.uk

Vodafone
tel: 07836 191191
www.vodafone.co.uk

VIRTUAL NETWORK OPERATORS

Fresh! (Value Telecom)
tel: 0800 049 0800
www.freshmobile.co.uk

Genie
tel: 0870 225 7879
www.mobile.genie.co.uk

Sainsbury's One
www.sainsburys.co.uk

Virgin Mobile
tel: 0845 600 0600
www.virgin.com/mobile

MOBILE PHONE MANUFACTURERS

For a full list, go to
www.ukmobilephonesguide.co.uk

Alcatel
www.alcatel.com

Ericsson
www.ericsson.co.uk

Motorola
www.motorola.co.uk

Nokia
www.nokia.co.uk

Siemens
www.siemens.com

HIGH-STREET RETAILERS

Which? says that when it last investigated which retailers give the best advice, the Carphone Warehouse and DX Communications (now part of O2) came out top. Comet came last.

The Carphone Warehouse
tel: 0808 1009 250
www.carphonewarehouse.co.uk

Comet
tel: 0845 6007 002
www.comet.co.uk

Dixons
tel: 08000 682868
www.dixons.co.uk

The Link
tel: 0500 222666
www.thelink.com

CONSUMER MAGAZINES

What Cellphone
tel: 01353 654411
www.what-cellphone.com

What Mobile
tel: 020 7878 1511
www.blah.com

ONLINE RETAILERS

You will often get a better deal via a website, but stick to established sites and do as much research as possible in magazines and on the high street before buying anything. Popular sites include:
www.buzz-mobile.co.uk
www.e2save.com
www.jungle.com
www.mobileshop.com
www.onestopphoneshop.co.uk
www.smalltalk.co.uk
www.talkingshop.co.uk
www.themobilerepublic.com
www.ukphoneshop.com

TARIFF-COMPARISON WEBSITES

www.buy.co.uk
www.uswitch.com

Which? will tell you which tariff it thinks you are best suited to. The test costs £9.95, and you can find the application form at
www.which.net/publicinterest/phone_tariffs.html

TELECOMS REGULATOR AND TRADE ASSOCIATION

Federation of Communications Services
tel: 020 8778 5656
www.fcs.org.uk

Oftel
tel: 020 7634 8700
www.oftel.org.uk

musical instruments

the basics

You've got an old tie knotted around your forehead. You've got a tennis racquet in one hand. You've got Queen's *Greatest Hits* in the other. Don't you think it's time you actually got yourself a guitar and learned how to play?

Air-guitar-wielding rockers and children embarking on a term of after-school music lessons have one thing in common: both would be best served by an instrument of their own.

The problem is that most musical instruments are extremely expensive, and as with gym memberships, most people rarely persist beyond the initial wave of enthusiasm. So, how can you get a good deal?

Establishing why you need an instrument is your first task. Have you been dusted by the nostalgia fairy and now regret snapping that flute in half after failing your Grade 1 exam? Are you a parent looking for a suitable beginner's model for your child that will not break the bank, but still produce a sweet enough sound? Or are you a keen amateur musician who is just looking for a good deal on a new instrument?

Whichever is the case, you'll need to buff up on what's currently available on the market. Musicians, like most keen hobbyists, are well served by specialist magazines and websites. Look through as many as you can to read reviews and to gauge prices before venturing into any music shops. It's also worth remembering that your local library is a great resource for music. Many will keep the specialist magazines you want and will often lend out what is normally expensive sheet music. A library's back issues will be especially helpful if you are looking up reviews for second-hand models. Alternatively, look online.

before you buy

It doesn't matter which instrument you're buying – piano, trumpet, guitar or piccolo – you should actually handle and test it before buying it. That may sound painfully obvious, but a large percentage of instruments bought today are via mail-order catalogues, the internet or classified ads. Even if you end up going down this route, try to test the same model at a local music shop to see if it's suitable. (Find the nearest shop via **www.musicadvertiser.com** or **www.yell.com**.)

You've been practising that lick for weeks now on your friend's guitar: now's the time to go and practise it on some display guitars down at the music shop. This can be as intimidating as a job interview, especially when you walk in and there's old Carlos 'guitar god' Santana in the corner showing off on the latest model before his loyal groupies, but it's a necessary rite of passage for any musician.

The best advice is not to try and go in with the intention of turning the amp up to 11 à la Spinal Tap and belting out the solo from *Stairway to Heaven* while down on your knees. It's best instead to leave the aspiring rock star at home and stick to something that will let you actually listen to the instrument's range and quality. Any instrument, if it's electric, will sound great on the shop's high-quality amps, and any instrument will sound great when demonstrated by Carlos (after all, that's what he's paid to do). In fact, if possible, don't let the instrument be demonstrated for you – you will not learn a thing other than the sales staff's favourite tune.

Whatever instrument you are trying out, don't be afraid to play it as loudly as you would at home. You will not be testing the instrument correctly if you meekly play a few notes in the corner. Blow, strum, drum, tinkle as freely as possible – and for a good ten minutes or more with each model. Some shops may have a practice room, which is ideal. Other than gauging the model's feel, sound and comfort, it is important to listen carefully for any flaws, such as fret buzz on guitars.

As with most purchases, it's best to have a friend come along for a second, unbiased opinion. Both of you should make notes on all the models you try out for future reference as, ideally, you will have tried several shops out before making a purchase.

Apply, too, some basic reverse sales psychology on the music shop's staff. Should you actually return to buy an instrument, you don't want to have given the sales staff a head start on price by letting them know what you are interested in, as music shop prices tend to be flexible. Therefore, never let on how much you have to spend when doing your research. Don't seem desperate to make a purchase: appear relaxed and knowledgeable. If you've done your homework beforehand, you will be able to engage in some of the

buying instruments for children

At some point during a child's schooling, most parents will face the dilemma of whether to invest in an expensive instrument. Should you spend hundreds of pounds on an instrument that could be abandoned in the corner of the child's bedroom as soon as the next fad usurps it?

The answer depends on the type of instrument, but if possible, try to borrow or rent an instrument for the first few crucial months of tuition. Many schools now offer this option; alternatively, try your local council's Music Service.

With some instruments, such as all string instruments, you shouldn't make any purchase, if possible, until the child can use a full-size version. There are many student models available for hire while the child is growing.

With woodwind and brass instruments, the advice seems to point towards buying new if possible once you are sure of a lasting interest, due to the low quality of second-hand student instruments.

When you do make a purchase, however, don't forget that you could be entitled to VAT exemption via your local education authority's Assisted Instrument Purchase Scheme. This is because instruments can be deemed a 'curriculum tool' if bought through the school, and thus not liable for VAT. This 17.5 per cent reduction could better the price offered by most music shops, so ask your school's music teacher for details, as the sale may need to go through them to qualify for the exemption.

You will certainly be thankful for any savings, considering that most music lessons cost upwards of about £90 a term. And then there are the orchestra fees (about £30 a term), the maintenance costs (up to £70 to re-pad a woodwind instrument every few years), and the travel costs of ferrying your children to lessons.

lingo and indicate that you are no mug when it comes to musical instruments. This will all pay off when you return with the cash (or more likely the credit card).

Other than the instrument itself, there are a few other things that you should be making enquiries about before heading for the till. After-sales care, insurance and warranties are important, particularly on more expensive or sensitive instruments. There's no point getting a good deal without extra touches such as these, so ask about the details when you are shopping around.

While some retailers may not wish to reduce prices, especially if the instrument is already on sale, many may throw in a few goodies when asked. If they won't budge on the price, try and get them to include things like wood polish, extra strings, tube cleaners, straps or a free music lesson. You will thank them for this when they remind you of all the other extras you will inevitably end up buying, such as a music stand, sheet music, stools, metronomes and the teach-yourself books.

Something that really should be part of the package is the instrument's carry-case. Don't be tricked into buying an instrument only to find out that the case is extra – an expensive extra at that. Make sure, too, that it is clear whether you are getting a soft or hard case, particularly when buying guitars. Be suspicious if a retailer just says that the case is included without offering further details.

And if you're buying any equipment that can be hooked up to a home computer, check to see whether the instrument's software and data ports are completely compatible with your machine. You should also ask whether you have adequate memory and processor speed on your machine. If you buy this instrument, are you going to have to buy a new computer to match?

buying from music shops

Not the cheapest way to buy an instrument, but you will get the personal touch that is so crucial for the uninitiated. Music shops also offer the huge advantage of being there for after-sales service and assistance.

Once you have completed your research, pick the shop that offers the best package, and if possible, take along cash for extra bargaining leverage. Some music shops will offer finance for expensive items such as pianos, but you will invariably be better off arranging your own loan via a bank or building society.

The most competitive retailers are likely to be located where music shops tend to cluster. The most famous area in the UK for music shops is Denmark Street – or Tin Pan Alley as it is also known – off London's Charing Cross Road, where, it is said, Noel Gallagher gets his guitars. The street even has its own website, **www.tinpanalley.co.uk**, to represent all the retailers.

buying from websites

In addition to helping you track down the conventional retailers who have an online presence, the internet can be the best way of buying instruments through 'drop ship' or factory-direct wholesalers. These are wholesalers who don't even bother with storing stock at a warehouse – they just deliver instruments to you straight from the manufacturers, and hence can offer you even better rates than mail-order and internet retailers.

Drop shippers popular with musicians include the US-based **www.musicyo.com**, but, as with all online transactions, stick to paying with a credit card, and research the delivery and customs and excise costs thoroughly. Additional questions that must have been answered satisfactorily include: what is the policy on returns? and do the manufacturers offer a full international guarantee?

second-hand versus new

The second-hand market for musical instruments is extremely buoyant. Just look at any *Loot* or newsagent's small ads notice board. The reason for this can probably be partly pinned on the 'faddish' nature of learning an instrument. While this often leads to many 'almost new' models being sold off cheaply, most instruments, like cars, lose up to 25 per cent of their original price as soon as the first note is played at home. Furthermore, with a bit of shopping around, new instruments can be competitively priced and offer the

expert view

Scott Rowley, editor of *Total Guitar*, offers his tips for buying a guitar. However, much of his advice makes sense when buying most other instruments too:

* Doing a bit of research will prepare you for when the salesperson starts to dazzle you with detail. In the world of guitars, for example, it's good to know the main differences between the best-known models – Stratocaster, Les Paul and Telecaster – but also stuff like the quality and price difference between Mexican and American-built Strats, as well as budget ranges like Squier and Epiphone.

* For guitars, check the frets by running your hand up the neck: rough edges are a sign of bad finishing. If it's an electric instrument, try the guitar unplugged first: it should still sound good. When plugged in (preferably in a soundproofed room so that you can really have a go without embarrassment), check that all the connections are good by switching pickups, and using the volume and control knobs. Look out for loose tuners or warped necks when buying second-hand (look down the neck to ensure it's not

bent – it may not be fixable later). Ask to borrow a guitar strap and put the guitar on to test the balance: if the headstock dips when you're not holding the guitar, the balance is off (not serious, but it could become a pain if you're going to do a lot of playing standing up).

* Ask if the guitar has been 'set up': many cheap guitars aren't even taken out of their boxes when they arrive at the shop, leading to bad 'action' (the distance between the strings and fret board). If not, ask if they'll do this for you as part of the sale, adjusting the action so that it's not too low (leading to string buzz as it vibrates against the frets) or too high (making it difficult to fret notes).

* It pays to have a clear idea of what music you're going to play before you commit to either an electric, steel-stringed acoustic or nylon-stringed guitar. You wouldn't believe how many people buy a nylon string and then can't understand why they don't sound anything like Metallica…

advantage of warranties and manuals, which will be especially important if buying computerized equipment such as a synthesizer.

The best place to check the current market prices for second-hand instruments is **www.prepal.com**. It constantly tracks websites and newsgroups for models, manufacturers and prices.

It is best, however, to have expensive instruments such as pianos checked out by a specialist before buying second-hand. When buying a piano, for example, something to look out for is whether it has been retuned in the last ten years. Any longer and it suggests neglect, so leave it alone. Antique pianos (older than eighty years) may look great as furniture, but unless it is a fully reconditioned, named model, it is unlikely to be better value than a new model, which, if cared for, will give you at least fifty years' service.

Whatever second-hand instrument you go for, make sure the seller hands over all the relevant manuals and paperwork.

PRIMARY RESOURCES

GENERAL MUSICIAN SITES

www.intermusic.com
www.musicadvertiser.com
www.musicgallery.co.uk
www.paythepiper.co.uk

ONLINE RETAILERS

www.chamberlainmusic.com
www.endeavourmusic.co.uk
www.dawkes.co.uk
www.dawsons.co.uk
www.djmmusic.com
www.forwoods.co.uk
www.guvnor.com
www.marsmusic.com
www.musicianshop.co.uk
www.musicalwarehouse.co.uk
www.musicyo.co.uk
www.mveshops.co.uk
www.normans.co.uk
www.pianosonline.co.uk
www.signetmusic.com
www.tinpanalley.co.uk
www.ukpianos.com
www.williams-music.co.uk

MUSIC TEACHERS

www.musicteachers.co.uk

SPECIALIST INSURANCE

British Reserve
tel: 0870 2400 303
www.britishreserve.co.uk

INSTRUMENT REVIEWS

www.harmony-central.com

LEADING MANUFACTURERS

Arbiter
www.arbiter.co.uk
Boosey & Hawkes
www.boosey.com
Fender
www.fender.co.uk
Korg
www.korg.co.uk

Gibson
www.gibson.com
Roland
www.roland.co.uk
Sabian
www.sabian.com
Stentor
www.stentor-music.com
Yamaha
www.yamaha-music.co.uk

TRADE ASSOCIATIONS

Music Industries Association
tel: 01483 223326
www.mia.org.uk

organic food

the basics

Here's your choice. On the one hand, you have an intensively farmed apple sprayed with pesticides that has just travelled thousands of miles to reach you. On the other, you have an organic apple, free from chemicals and locally grown. It's not difficult to work out which most people would choose, and the answer explains why the organic food sector has grown into a £1 billion industry in the last few years.

From the point of view of your health, the attraction of organic food currently appears irresistible. After a decade or more of food scares, organic food seemingly offers a safe haven. Organic food also appears to be kinder to the environment than factory-farmed produce and looks to offer animals kinder living conditions. But above all, the consumer is drawn – although it is yet to be proved – by the offer of better taste and better nutrition.

However, there are two factors that prevent an all-out consumer stampede towards organic: price and shelf life. Organic food can be up to twice the price of regular supermarket offerings and generally doesn't last as long, due to its lack of preservatives. This doesn't fit in very well with our modern desire for convenience and 'value for money'.

Of course, the organic lobby would argue that, given its perceived benefits, organic food is worth every penny. Some things, after all, are almost beyond price. But if you have made the life choice that organic is the way forward – even if only for a handful of products such as baby food – you will want to make sure that you are getting exactly what you have paid for.

proving it's organic

The term 'organic' is actually a legal term regulated by the EEC. It is an offence for manufacturers or retailers to use the term unless a product has been certified by a recognized organic agency. Confusingly perhaps, there are a handful of such agencies in the UK, all of which are registered and monitored by the government's organic watchdog, the United Kingdom Register of Organic Food Standards (UKROFS). To add to the confusion, UKROFS itself also acts as a small-time certifying agency.

The Soil Association is the best known of these agencies and certifies up to 70 per cent of all the organic food produced in the UK. It probably has the most rigorous standards, but all the other agencies ensure that their standards easily meet the minimum legal requirements. (There is certainly no implication that any one agency is 'better' than any other – it is just that some focus on different concerns.)

The basic premise of organic food is that it has been grown or reared on an organic farm. These farms gain their status by going through a two-year conversion period, in which they let their fields rest by preventing the use of nearly all chemical fertilizer or pesticides. Once converted, the farm then promises to remain largely free from such chemicals and ensures that animals are fed with organic feed. Farmers will also promise that animals are kept and slaughtered in a humane manner. The ultimate organic farm is a 'closed cycle', one in which the fields are fertilized using manure from the farm's livestock, which are in turn fed with feed grown on the farm.

When you look at a product that claims to be organic, in most cases you will see the symbol of an organic agency, but this isn't a legal requirement. It is required, however, that the labelling displays an agency code, for example 'Organic Certification: UK 1'. The agency codes are as listed here [◁]. (NB: UK8 has not yet been

---

organic agency codes

UK 1	United Kingdom Register of Organic Food Standards (UKROFS)
UK 2	Organic Farmers and Growers
UK 3	Scottish Organic Producers Association
UK 4	Organic Food Federation
UK 5	The Soil Association
UK 6	Biodynamic Agricultural Association
UK 7	Irish Organic Farmers and Growers Association
UK 9	The Organic Trust
UK 10	CMi Certification

allocated to Food Certification (Scotland) Ltd because, although there are recognized private standards for salmon farming (as allowed by EC regulations), fish products are not yet covered by EC rules.)

As you can see, home-grown organic food standards are policed vigorously. The confusion and doubts begin to creep in when you consider that the UK imports up to 70 per cent of the organic produce that it consumes. Is there a common global definition of what constitutes an 'organic' product?

Sadly, the answer is no. In fact, in the US alone there are ninety certification agencies. Fortunately, EU standards are consistent, and member countries now boast their own national agencies like UKROFS, but the only body that tries to regulate the entire global organic market is the International Federation of Organic Agriculture Movements, based in Germany. It says that it monitors some 730 organizations in ninety-seven countries, but these numbers just illustrate how diverse the standards are.

Fortunately, any organic food imported into the EU must come from a country or importer recognized as applying the same standards. But as with any mass market, the majority of control is based on trust. It is therefore best to try and buy organic food from the nearest available local source. You will, of course, be cutting back on the distribution mileage, the so-called 'food miles' or 'farm-to-fork' distance.

When you are looking at the label to find out the food's origin, remember too that just because something is labelled as being organic, it isn't necessarily 100 per cent organic. Manufacturers are allowed to use up to 5 per cent non-organic, agriculturally-derived ingredients in a product. If a product contains between 70 and 95 per cent organic ingredients, it cannot be called organic. Instead, its label must list each organic ingredient individually.

Food with less than 70 per cent organic ingredients must not, by law, make any reference to the word 'organic' on its label. However, if a farmer is in the process of converting to organic status, they can say 'product under conversion to organic farming' on the label.

box schemes

Possibly the best-known way to buy organic food is via a box scheme. Pay between £5 and £20 a week and someone will knock on your door clutching a cardboard box stuffed full of delicious, seasonal, organic fruit and veg. The scheme has many advantages: the food is incredibly fresh (the wet mud is always a giveaway); you are invariably supporting a local farmer; you are enjoying seasonal food; and it is even more convenient than picking something up from the corner shop.

The old perception of box schemes was that you got what you were told and that invariably meant something as uncompromising as two carrots, a potato and a bunch of leeks. This notion has progressed somewhat, and like milkmen, box schemes will now deliver a whole range of additional goods including meat, wine and dairy produce. And if you are unable to be at home for the delivery, most schemes will happily drop off the box at a mutually convenient place like a neighbour's or a community centre. They may even leave it under a hedge in your garden if that's more convenient.

The range of produce is dictated by seasonal availability, which leads to wonderful variety throughout most months, but in the spring months, many box schemes are suspended due to the so-called 'hungry gap'. This is caused by the lack of available produce during these key growing months, and leads many box schemes to compensate by using imported goods. Whatever the time of year, though, most box schemes offer a set range of options, though most will cater to the occasional request based on individual preferences and dislikes (broccoli, for example).

When you are choosing which scheme to use, spend a bit of time investigating the origins of the scheme's produce as well as comparing prices. Of course, they must be accredited by an organic agency, but you should try to find one that sources its produce from as near to you as possible to reduce the food miles. Many schemes also now arrange open days at their source farms to encourage you to see the produce growing (great for kids). The scheme should also automatically recycle all the cardboard boxes.

The Soil Association (see 'primary resources') provides a list of all the box schemes around the country via its Organic Directory, which can either be bought as a book or viewed online.

farmers' markets

This may sound like something from an idyllic rural vision, but, like box schemes, farmers' markets are booming. The idea is simple: if you won't go to farmers to buy their produce, they will come to you. This usually takes the form of a weekly gathering in a car park, field or community hall in which local farmers will sell their wares directly to you (for surprisingly low prices in most cases, as the middleman has been eliminated).

Again, freshness is the key selling point, but don't assume that all the produce is organic – far from it. As with everywhere else, the same rules apply: they must be accredited by an organic agency. Organic farmers will display a certificate on their stall, and if they say they are in the process of converting to organic, ask how they are going about it and who they plan to register with.

For a full list of farmers' markets, contact the National Association of Farmers' Markets (see 'primary resources').

supermarkets

If we are ever to achieve a totally organic weekly shop, the supermarkets are going to have to be in on it, too. The top five UK supermarkets account for a majority of all our food purchases, but although they have all enthusiastically begun to promote organic ranges, most people would argue that prices still remain too high to make a full conversion.

The chains claim that their prices simply reflect the extra costs needed to produce organic food, and that profit margins are the same as all their other food, but with only 3 per cent of all farms in the UK having converted to organic, the supermarkets are still having to import the bulk of their organic food from abroad, which is costly and anathema to the general principals of organics. Consumer power is the only way that supermarkets and farmers are going to be

ethics watch: all health food is organic, right?

According to researchers at *Ethical Consumer* magazine, the health food sector, as you would expect, has a strong presence of ethical companies pursuing the organic principle. There are notable exceptions, however. Quorn, for example, belongs to the genetic engineering multinational AstraZeneca. Solgar vitamins belong to American Home Products, a company criticized for violating the international code governing the marketing of breast-milk substitutes. And Enjoy is owned by the venture capital fund Doughty Hanson, which is involved with the military and the nuclear industry. For more information, visit www.ethicalconsumer.org or call 0161 226 2929.

convinced that UK shoppers are serious in the long term about going organic, so if you are serious about it, keep persisting. Prove to them it's not just another food fad we're going through.

expert view

The environment benefits greatly from organic food production, says Zac Goldsmith, editor of the *Ecologist* magazine, yet around 75 per cent of the organic food eaten in the UK is imported, and only 3 per cent of land in the UK is organic. So the UK environment is losing out. Not to mention our farmers and our economy.

So you can do your bit to increase organic production here in the UK by:

- Signing up to the Organic Targets Campaign that aims to have 30 per cent of land organic by 2010. Thousands of individuals and the majority of backbench MPs in Parliament already support this vital campaign but the government is still wavering. Find out more at www.sustainweb.org.

- Ensuring your own MP has signed up to Early Day Motion 366 in support of the organic targets campaign.

- Joining a major rally in support of organic farming. Find out more at www.sustainweb.org.

- Buying local organic produce wherever possible, preferably from farmers' markets, or directly from farmers themselves through box schemes certified by the Soil Association.

- Lobbying the supermarkets, if necessary through boycotts, to favour local producers and pay farmers fair prices for their goods.

PRIMARY RESOURCES

ORGANIC CERTIFICATION AGENCIES

Biodynamic Agricultural Association
tel: 01453 759501
www.anth.org.uk/biodynamic

CMi Certification
tel: 01993 885645
www.cmi-plc.com

Food Certification (Scotland)
tel: 01463 222251
www.foodcertificationscotland.co.uk

International Federation of Organic Agriculture Movements (Germany)
tel: (+49) 6853 919890
www.ifoam.org

Irish Organic Farmers and Growers Association
tel: (+353) 0506 32563
www.irishorganic.ie

Organic Farmers and Growers
tel: 01743 440512
www.organicfarmers.uk.com

Organic Food Federation
tel: 01362 637314
www.orgfoodfed.com

The Organic Trust (Ireland)
tel: (+353) 1 853 0271
www.iol.ie/~organic/trust.html

Scottish Organic Producers Association
tel: 01786 458090
www.sopa.org.uk

The Soil Association
tel: 0117 914 2400
www.soilassociation.org

United Kingdom Register of Organic Food Standards (UKROFS)
tel: 020 7238 5605
www.defra.gov.uk/farm/organic

OTHER ORGANIC ORGANIZATIONS

Henry Doubleday Research Association (Europe's largest organic research membership organization)
tel: 0247 630 3517
www.hdra.org.uk

Sustain, the alliance for better food and farming
tel: 020 7837 1228
www.sustainweb.org

BOOKS

Green Cuisine, by Anna Ross (Green Peppercorn, £7.99)

Henrietta Green's Food Lovers' Guide to Britain, by Henrietta Green (BBC Consumer Publishing, £10.99)

Organic, by Sophie Grigson and William Black (Headline, £25)

The Organic Directory, edited by Clive Litchfield (Green Books, £7.95; www.theorganicdirectory.com)

Planet Organic: Organic Living, by Lynda Brown (Dorling Kindersley, £14.99)

MAGAZINES

Country Smallholding
tel: 01799 540922
www.countrysmallholding.com

Digest, the quarterly magazine from Sustain
tel: 020 7837 1228
www.sustainweb.org

The Ecologist
tel: 01795 414963
www.theecologist.org

Ethical Consumer
tel: 0161 226 2929
www.ethicalconsumer.org

Living Earth, the magazine of the Soil Association
tel: 0117 929 0661
www.soilassociation.org

Natural Products (organic trade magazine)
tel: 01903 817303
www.naturalproducts.co.uk

FARMERS' MARKETS

London Farmers' Markets
tel: 020 7704 9659
www.lfm.org.uk

National Association of Farmers' Markets
tel: 01225 787914
www.farmersmarkets.net

Regional listings of farmers' markets
www.thefoody.com/regionalfm.html

Scottish Association of Farmers' Markets
www.scottishfarmersmarkets.co.uk

ORGANIC RETAILERS AND BOX SCHEMES

Absolut Organic
tel: 01386 834499
www.absolutorganic.co.uk

Farmaround Organic
tel: 020 7627 8066
www.farmaround.co.uk

The Fresh Food Co
tel: 020 8969 0351
www.freshfood.co.uk

Graig Farm Organics
tel: 01597 851655
www.graigfarm.co.uk

Iorganic
tel: 020 7692 4966
www.iorganic.co.uk

The Organic Delivery Company
tel: 020 7739 8181
www.organicdelivery.co.uk

The Organic Shop
tel: 0845 674 4000
www.theorganicshop.co.uk

Farmaround Organic
020 7627 8066
www.farmaround.co.uk

Organics Direct
tel: 020 8545 7676
www.organicsdirect.co.uk

Real Food Direct
tel: 0118 956 7700
www.realfooddirect.co.uk

The Real Meat Company
tel: 01985 840562
www.realmeat.co.uk

Simply Organic
tel: 0845 1000 444
www.simplyorganic.net

POPULAR ORGANIC FOOD BRANDS

BabyOrganix
www.babyorganix.co.uk

Hipp
www.hipp.co.uk

Pure Organics
www.organics.org

Simply Organic
www.simplyorganic.co.uk

Whole Earth
www.earthfoods.co.uk

pets

the basics

Over 60 per cent of UK households are home to some kind of pet, but despite our much-celebrated love of animals, the RSPCA picks up around 150,000 discarded pets a year. So what are we doing wrong when it comes to choosing a suitable pet?

The allure of a pet is a large part of the problem. For many, the appeal is companionship, and a loved pet often becomes an equal member of a family. It is also proven that pets are good for our health – so much so that doctors often allow dogs and cats to visit patients in hospital. They help to lower blood pressure, can effectively reduce stress and many make sure that we maintain a basic routine of exercise. All this sounds positive, but sadly many people fail to see beyond the face of an adorable puppy or kitten and forget what a huge commitment owning a pet can be.

By buying a dog or cat, for example, you are committing yourself to about fifteen years of costs and responsibilities. A horse will live even longer, so try to think of it as being as big a commitment as having a child. Can you afford the £700 a year that a dog will, on average, cost you in food and vet's bills? The cost of a cat over its lifetime will amount to about £8,000. Are you prepared to spend several months house-training a pet and paying for spoiled carpets or scratched furniture? Do you have the time in the day to attend to a pet's needs?

Before making a decision about whether you get a pet, let alone choosing which breed or species you want, ask yourself the following questions:

* *are you a suitable pet owner?* Be tough with yourself when answering this question. Every family member, no matter how old, must be consulted (never surprise anyone, especially a child, with a pet as a gift), and you must all decide whether you are prepared to care for a pet. Discuss who would have which duties. If you live alone, can you care for all the pet's needs? Are you only ever at home at night and at weekends? Ideally, you should temporarily experience someone else's pet before any purchase. Will anyone you know let you 'babysit' their pet for a few hours or a weekend? Research the species and breed on the internet and at the library, and speak to a local vet or animal society for advice on what to expect from the animal. Remember, too, that if you are pregnant you don't want to be near cat litter, for example, so ask your doctor for additional advice about the suitability of pets.

* *do you live in a suitable environment for a pet?* Just because you may own lots of land and have a big house, it doesn't necessarily mean that your home is automatically suited to a pet. Are you adjacent to a busy road, electrical substation or other properties with lots of animals? Will all your neighbours welcome a new resident to the area? Do you live near protected wildlife? If you live in a built-up area, is there a large local park to, for example, walk a dog twice a day? Residents of flats, especially if they are above the ground floor, should think hard about their choice of pet.

* *where will your animal go when you're away on holiday?* Do you have neighbours or relatives who would be willing to look after your pet when you go away? The cost of paying for temporary care is expensive and most pets are kept for long hours in cages with little scope for exercise.

* *do you have allergies?* It's worth getting tested if you have never lived with a pet before. Ask your doctor or a vet.

* *are you even allowed to have a pet?* If you are renting your home, you may be surprised to know that many rental contracts have a 'no pets' clause. Read the small print. Some contracts

expressly state which species you can and cannot own. You may have to get written permission from your neighbouring tenants for pets such as dogs and cats. Rodents are also often restricted. Most landlords, however, will have little complaint about a fish tank.

which animal?

Once you establish which kind of pet is suitable, you can begin to narrow down your preferred species and breed. But still keep asking yourself whether you're suitable for every choice.

What size of animal do you want? Could you handle a large dog? Would you get bored of a tropical fish? Consider, too, each animal's levels of activity. Find out what would be a good entry-level example of a species. For first-time bird owners, for example, finches are easy to care for and have an average lifespan of about five to eight years. Canaries and budgerigars can live up to the age of fifteen, and a large parrot can live as long as thirty years.

If you have limited time to commit to your pet, you should possibly choose something like a hamster, rabbit, fish or bird, but pay particular consideration to the animal's well-being and quality of environment if it is to be contained in a cage, tank or hutch. Spend as much as you can afford on what, after all, is not just its home, but its world.

What about noise levels? Ask what you can expect from each animal. Did you know, for example, that a male canary sings, unlike female canaries? When did you last go into a quiet pet shop? Find out about the animal's expected habits. Many animals lose hair or skin, too. Are you prepared to constantly be following your pet with a vacuum cleaner wherever it goes?

Dismiss any idea of getting an exotic or wild pet simply because they are rare and unusual. The 'designer pet' market is notoriously murky and is often shamed by revelations of cruelty and illegal smuggling. And don't dismiss older animals. They may not look cute and innocent, but an older animal is much more manageable and will require less house-training than, for example, a puppy. Contrary to popular myth, you can teach an old dog new tricks.

Finally, visit as many animal shows as you can to help you make the correct choice. Talk to owners about what to expect. Check with the relevant animal society to see where the nearest shows are, and consider volunteering at a local pet rescue centre. You never know, you may even meet your new best friend.

buying the pet

How and where you buy a pet is a contentious matter (see 'ethics watch'). The RSPCA unites with most animal welfare groups in advising that you should always try to get a pet via an animal rescue centre first before considering breeders or pet shops. For every pet bought from a pet shop or breeder, an animal will have to be put down at a rescue centre. The RSPCA also advises that you shouldn't buy an animal out of pity alone and that you should never buy a kitten or puppy from pet shops, as they're often taken away from their mothers at an early age and mixed with other litters where they may catch diseases.

Research and investigate the reputation of any pet shop you consider. Look for members of the Pet Care Trust (see 'primary resources'). Even the large, nationwide pet shop chains need careful research. The country's largest pet shop chain, Pets At Home (which recently incorporated Petsmart), received high-profile criticism towards the end of 2001 from BBC1's *Watchdog* programme for animal welfare related issues. (Go to **www.bbc.co.uk/watchdog** and search for 'Pets At Home' to read about the programme's investigation.)

Try to avoid buying pets via newspaper ads or from 'the man in the pub' – sadly, still a very common route. Unless you can guarantee via references that the vendor is reputable and has the animal's interest at heart, it is best avoided.

Wherever you buy your pet, make sure you get a very detailed receipt complete with feeding and care instructions. Your consumer rights ensure, just as with any other purchase, that your pet should be of 'satisfactory quality' and 'as described'. You are entitled to expect your new pet not to suddenly develop an illness as soon as you take ownership. And if you're buying a dog or cat, seriously considered getting it neutered to help alleviate the Malthusian nightmare of pet overpopulation that confronts organizations such as the RSPCA.

Arrange for the animal to be microchipped and for the unique code to be placed on the national PetLog database, which boasts the details of more than 450,000 animals. A small microchip the size of a grain of rice will be injected just under the pet's skin, and for about £20 the details will be recorded. If your pet gets lost or is stolen, a simple scan will reveal the animal's true identity and owner.

To minimize costly vet bills it is highly recommended that you insure your pet. It is estimated that only 15 per cent of people bother to get pet insurance, but with costs running into the thousands for many animals it is wise to get cover. Insurance costs clearly vary, but monthly premiums can range from £4 for a rabbit to well over £30 for a horse. Cats and dogs usually cost between £5 and £15 a month to insure. As ever, shop around for the best premium, but check details such as the amount of excess.

Lastly, prepare your home for your pet before you pick it up.

buying from a breeder

It is important to spend time tracking down someone responsible. Get as many referrals as you can: ask friends, ask local vets, phone breed clubs and associations, and speak to your local rescue centre if they can't provide an animal for you. Once you have a shortlist, ask the breeder if you can visit them before making any decisions. Any good breeder will not object to this. In fact, they should actively encourage it, as they should be as keen to find a good home for their animals as you are to find a good breeder.

What to look for during your visit:
(NB: This advice is for buying a dog, but large parts are pertinent for most species.)

* Ask to look around their premises. Be wary of a breeder that is not keen to show you all their facilities. What are they hiding?

* Look for an animal that is energetic, inquisitive and happy in human company. Avoid ones that are timid and anxious or aggressive

towards humans. Timid puppies may look cute, but it could mean the dog is fearful and hence likely to become aggressive in later life.

◈ Ask to see the animal's parents. You want to see puppies with their mothers and, ideally, their fathers, raised in comfort with littermates and with ample human contact.

◈ Request the names of owners of related dogs and, if a pedigree, for a detailed family tree. Contact these owners for information about their dogs' behaviour, training history and health patterns.

◈ Ask how many breeds they have available. Responsible breeders tend to stick to one or two breeds. Be wary of breeders who have a variety of breeds available for selection.

◈ Ask about guarantees and pedigree papers. Quality breeders, ostensibly animal-lovers rather than business people, should be willing to take back an animal for any reason.

ethics watch

People for the Ethical Treatment of Animals (Peta) urges those who are buying a 'companion animal' to remember the following points:

'Puppy mills' breed thousands of dogs every year in deplorable conditions to supply disreputable pet stores, compounding the overpopulation crisis. There are far too many homeless animals in shelters that are waiting for a loving family.

It takes patience, love and time to train animals – even this is not always enough.

Declawing cats is cruel, so make sure there are scratch posts available. Be prepared to keep cats indoors unless you are accompanying them on a leash (with a harness). Outside, cats are vulnerable to cruel people, cars and disease, and may get lost or even stolen. Cats may also kill birds, rabbits and other wildlife when outside; it's their natural instinct.

Fragile tropical fish suffer miserably when forced to spend their lives enclosed in glass. Robbed of their natural habitat, denied the space to roam, they must swim and re-swim the same empty cubic inches. Many of these delicate animals die in transport.

Never, ever buy a bird from a pet store. Birds have complicated needs that are rarely met in a home environment. Exotic birds can live for twenty to seventy years, and the stress of confinement can lead to neurotic behaviour and self-mutilation. If you are adopting birds, do you have an area where they can fly freely? Birds should always be kept with at least one other member of their own species.

And finally, here are a few Peta websites that discuss further companion animal issues:
www.fixcats.com
www.helpinganimals.com
www.helppuppies.com
Contact Peta (tel: 020 8870 3966, www.petaeurope.org).

PRIMARY RESOURCES

ANIMAL RESCUE CENTRES

Battersea Dogs' Home
tel: 020 7622 3626
www.dogshome.org

The Blue Cross adoption centres
tel: 01993 822651
www.thebluecross.org.uk
Eleven adoption centres
nationwide. Rehouse all pets.
Also run free Animal hospitals for
pet owners on low incomes, and
two equine rehabilitation centres.

Cats' Protection shelters
tel: 01403 221919
www.cats.org.uk

Index of Animal Rescue Centres
(website that lists dozens of UK
rescue centres)
www.animalsanctuaries.co.uk

The Mayhew Animal Home
tel: 020 8969 0178 ext 21 or 22
www.mayhewanimalhome.org

**National Canine Defence League
rehousing scheme**
tel: 020 7837 0006
www.ncdl.org.uk

The RSPCA animal centres
tel: 0870 3335 999
www.rspca.org.uk

UK Animal Rescuers (directory of
UK rescue centres)
www.animalrescuers.co.uk

PET SHOPS

The Pet Care Trust
Member pet shops display the
trust's blue logo and sign up to its
ethical code of practice, in
addition to holding mandatory
local authority pet sellers'
licences. The trust also maintains
the Puppy Index, a national
database of reputable dog
breeders. Contact the trust to find
your nearest member pet shop.
tel: 01234 273933
www.petcare.org.uk
For a directory of UK pet shops
and breeders visit
www.ukpets.co.uk

PET ASSOCIATIONS

The British Bird Council
tel: 0121 476 5999
www.britishbirdcouncil.com

The British Horse Society
tel: 08701 202244
www.bhs.org.uk

The British Rabbit Council
www.thebrc.org

The Feline Advisory Bureau
tel: 01747 871872
www.fabcats.org

**The International Herpetological
Society** (snakes)
www.international-herp-society.
co.uk

The Kennel Club
tel: 0870 606 6750
www.the-kennel-club.org.uk

The National Fancy Rat Society
www.nfrs.org

The National Gerbil Society
www.gerbils.co.uk

National Hamster Council
www.hamsters-uk.org

Ornamental Fish
www.ornamentalfish.org

PET SECURITY

The National PetLog Database
tel: 0870 606 6751
www.petlog.org.uk

PET INSURANCE

E&L Insurance
tel: 0870 742 3710
www.eandl.co.uk

PetPlan
tel: 0800 072 7000
www.petplan.co.uk

Pinnacle
tel: 020 8207 9000
www.pinnacle.co.uk/pet

Tesco Pet Insurance
tel: 0845 300 2200
www.tesco.com/finance/pet/pet.htm

plants

the basics

Gardening is more than a national obsession: it's an addiction. It is estimated that over eighteen million of us are keen gardeners and that thirty million of us buy at least one plant every year. That means that garden centres are ringing up about three billion pounds' worth of business a year. Now that's a lot of hardy perennials.

Our extraordinary enthusiasm for all things horticultural is reflected in book sales, too. Many would be hard pressed to name the second-biggest selling author of the last decade. Catherine Cookson comes in at number one, but close behind is Dr Dave Hessayon. 'Who?' you're probably asking. Hessayon is the author of the *Expert Gardening* guides, which have sold over forty-two million copies worldwide. The most popular in the series, *The House Plant Expert*, has sold over eleven million copies and is possibly the biggest-selling reference book of all time, after the Bible. (Future tie-in: The Garden of Eden, as landscaped by *Ground Force*?)

But while we may be champion roses when it comes to our collective knowledge about plants and gardening, we are still shrinking violets and wallflowers when it comes to bagging a quality bargain down at the garden centre. This is surprising, considering how many gardening programmes now fill the airwaves, but while they may tell us the differences between a camellia and a chrysanthemum, they often fail to tell us where and how to buy plants.

garden centres

A weekend trip down to the local garden centre is still the preferred method of buying plants for the vast majority of us. Most towns now have a garden centre, and while we may bemoan some of their exorbitant prices, they are still perceived as the easiest way to pick up a plant. The expert knowledge provided by the staff and the convenience of a one-stop shopping environment are still the primary reasons given for why garden centre sales continue to boom. Ask that question on an Easter weekend and views might change, but, by and large, garden centres are still the best overall option we have.

The first step to the smart buy, however, is to plan your trip a few weeks, if not months, in advance. Don't fall for the common mistake of the impulse buy. Many people look out of the window, see the sorry state of their neglected garden, wait for a spot of sunshine, and then dash down to the garden centre for a quick remedy. This is a bread-and-butter customer for garden centres.

Think about the time of year and work out what your garden really needs. Get hold of the Royal Horticultural Society's *Plant Finder* annual guide (£12.99, updated every May and also searchable free online). It lists thousands of different plant varieties and, crucially, tells you the nearest dealer that stocks them, saving you having to run around. And while you're at it, work out exactly how many plants you need. It's a common mistake to buy too many or too few plants.

When it comes to house plants, it is especially important to have considered whether you have the right environment for a particular plant. Most problems come from bad light conditions, so always check to see if a plant requires extra light, such as the light cast by an east- or south-facing window. As a rule, darker-coloured leaves tend to require less light than plants with variegated leaves. Perhaps try buying smaller plants rather than fully-grown ones, to give the plant a chance to grow into its new home. Also consider whether you are an under-waterer or an over-waterer and find plants to suit.

The timing of your visit to a garden centre is very important. Spring, particularly over Easter, is the busiest period, so try to plan ahead and avoid this time if possible. If not, avoid weekends at all costs. Unfortunately, but understandably, spring is when most plants are delivered to garden centres, so it may also be the best time to find the freshest and healthiest plants. Gardeners often complain that garden centres are reluctant to stock hardies in the autumn (the best time for planting) and beyond, but with the costs of storing and maintaining plants, many garden centres are now forcing the whole-sale nurseries to supply them with summer and autumn flowering hardies only between Easter and the August bank holiday. This is a shame, as gardeners often feel that autumn should be the best time to buy plants.

Ideally, you should be heading for independent, local garden centres if you want expert advice. If you want bargains, then head for the supermarket chains like B&Q and Homebase. But while they may be unbeatable on price, the quality of advice offered is generally much lower. Garden centres will also know your local growing conditions much better.

Try to avoid garden centres located in the centre of large towns and cities, too. The prices are generally much higher and you may find the range quite limiting. If you can, head out of town. When you arrive and start to look around, remember that garden centres are experts at snaring the impulse buyer. When was the last time you popped out for some compost and came back with the boot loaded with all manner of gardening paraphernalia you were convinced you needed? Many will design the store's layout with this in mind, so look out for the following 'honeypots':

* **the 'Plant of the Year':** The gardening industry seems obsessed with promoting the latest, trendy variety, which often comes with a snappy designer name. They will often have the endorsement of a gardening celebrity and a price to match. Do you really need it, or is it just a marketing gimmick?

* **hot spots:** Like all supermarkets, garden centres place things they want to sell in so-called 'hot spots', such as by the entrance or at the end of an aisle. With their high-visibility positioning, hot-spot items can see a 500 per cent increase in sales.

* **carpets:** An odd one, admittedly, but many shops use coloured carpets to 'guide' us towards things they want us to buy. Garden

centres often use green carpets to guide us towards plants, and brown carpets to guide us towards their non-gardening items.

* *loaded trolleys:* How many times have you picked up a plant from a trolley that seems to be standing there awaiting a member of staff to unload it onto nearby shelves? You think you're getting the freshest plants, don't you? Well, often this is another sales technique, as garden centres know how much their customers want to buy the freshest stock available.

* *latin-less labels:* Garden centres believe that customers perceive that a plant with a long Latin name is somehow going to be harder to grow than one with a nice friendly name. Again, like the Plant of the Year, it's another marketing ploy aimed at getting you to buy the plant varieties they want you to buy, rather than what you might be after.

* *'hiding' popular items:* How many times have you gone looking for a big seller like compost only to find it right at the back of the shop? The garden centres aren't stupid; they're making you walk past all their other tempting goods before you get there.

* *mass displays:* A large display of one type of seasonal plant gives off the appearance that it is a required buy. It also looks like a bulk buy and, hence, a bargain. It's an old sales trick, but one of the best.

This may appear to be a cynical way in which to view a garden centre, but remember that it is estimated that up to a third of all plant sales are achieved on impulse buys. Even if you know exactly what you want and have done all the right research, you will want to make sure you are buying the best quality for your money. Run this checklist through your head when you're inspecting plants:

* Are the plants packed too close to one another? Look for good colour and healthy foliage that has had room to breathe. Bushes, for example, should have at least three stems, with branches spread equally all around them. Perennials should have more than one stem.

* Is the plant pot-bound? In other words, are the roots tightly packed and coming out of the bottom of the plant's pot? If so,

avoid. Also avoid plants that have any weeds in the pots. It's a sign the plant may have been neglected.

* Have the roots and buds of deciduous plants been protected from moisture loss and breakage with adequate covering?

* Is the plant in bloom? Don't be tempted to buy plants that are flowering. Instead, select plants that have healthy, dormant buds. Also avoid plants that are too leggy or wilted.

* If it is a tree, is the root ball too soft and saggy or pancake-shaped? It should be firm and secure.

* Is there any sign of leaf spot, black spot, mildew or mites? It is advisable to quarantine your new plants from others at home for a couple of weeks anyway, but look out for things such as cobwebs on the foliage or small white eggs under the leaves.

Apart from running through this checklist, assess the quality of the staff. Ask them whether a particular plant is suitable for your soil type and growing conditions. Look to see whether they are attentive and willing to help. Are there staff caring for the plants, as well as the customers? If they are, it should be a sign of a professionally run garden centre that has a passion for its plants.

On your way to the garden centre, you may spot someone selling plants from the roadside or at a car boot sale. It is generally advised not to buy plants from the roadside, as you have no way of knowing their origin and how well they have been cared for. They may have been grown from inferior seed, or have been rejected by a garden centre and be harbouring pests or disease.

It is worth considering flower shows and fairs, however (see 'primary resources'). There are the famous ones such as the Royal Horticultural Society's annual shows at Chelsea, Hampton Court and Tatton Park in Cheshire. There's also BBC Gardeners' World Live in Birmingham and the spring and autumn shows at Malvern in Worcestershire. It is unlikely you will find many bargains, but you will be surrounded by people with a true passion for their plants, who should have good local tips on where to buy.

Don't forget that large horticultural shows are also held abroad. There are two big fairs each year at the beautiful chateau at Saint-

ethics watch: 'green' fingers?

Gardening may seem to be the perfect hobby for the environmentalist, but sadly, many of the common products we use in the garden are far from green. It is obvious that most chemical pesticides used in the garden cannot be eco-friendly, but it isn't widely known that one of the prime culprits is compost – possibly a garden centre's top seller.

Whenever you buy some, make sure that it is clearly labelled 'peat-free'. Garden centres are coming round to the fact that peat extraction is extremely damaging to peat bogs and their wildlife, and are stocking more and more alternative composts that are made from wood chippings, bark and even composted sewage. This is not to say that the compost is organic – look for extra labelling if that's important to you – but it is an important step for an industry that sells 2 million cubic metres of peat a year.

And put down that feed you're about to buy. Research seems to suggest that feed makes little difference to a plant's performance – in most cases, it's down to the quality of the soil. Most plant feed is packed full of nasty nitrates and other chemicals commonly used in fertilizers, so try to avoid it.

Jean de Beauregard just outside Paris – hardy plants at the beginning of April, and fruit and vegetables in November. For three days in the middle of June, there is also a large plant sale at Huis Bingerden, near Arnhem in Holland. Up to sixty nurseries have stalls here, and you'll find more than just the odd tulip variety too.

And if you really mean business, you may wish to join a local gardening club. There are hundreds around the country, and many secure large discounts from manufacturers by bulk-buying, as well as providing advice and holding regular meetings. Look in your local paper or contact the Royal Horticultural Society to find the club nearest to you.

mail order and websites

Having your plants and seeds delivered through the post is becoming increasingly popular. Obviously, you have to know what you want and can't really expect any knowledgeable advice, but for convenience and cost, home delivery is hard to beat. It's also a great way of finding rare plants and seeds.

As ever, stick to the bigger, well-known firms, particularly when buying via a website. Try to find catalogues and sites that accompany their lists of plants and seeds with plenty of detail. You want to know the full name of your plants, their height, spread, flower and fruit size, how long they will flower for, how to grow them, their ideal growing conditions and what the drawbacks could be.

Remember, though, that some firms do not always dispatch your order immediately. They may wait for the stock to be grown or it may be delayed by bad weather. To avoid any disappointment, make sure you are told when you place your order whether you are being placed on a waiting list or are being sent a substitute plant.

Seeds are particularly good to buy online or via a catalogue. They're cheap to send and often arrive fresher than buying from a garden centre, as it is less likely that they will have spent long periods in storage. Don't, however, bulk-buy seeds. They don't last for ages as is commonly believed (up to two years maximum), and it will prove a false economy.

Be careful about buying plants and seeds from websites based abroad. While you are generally allowed to import plants and seeds from any EU country, there are severe restrictions on importing from elsewhere. It is best to check the DEFRA website for details beforehand (www.defra.gov.uk/planth/phindx.htm), as some plants may need an expensive phytosanitary certificate to clear customs.

A common problem when having plants delivered is making sure that the delivery firm arrives at a convenient time. You don't want plants being left on the doorstep in freezing or sweltering temperatures, so try and arrange a good time when placing an order, and if

---

expert view

Seven top tips from Rosemary Ward of *Gardening Which?*:

* Always buy hardy cyclamen as plants rather than dry corms (globular underground stem bases), so you can pick the prettiest foliage patterns.

* Young evergreens are often rather tender, and growers tend to cosset them in polytunnels, so autumn planting can be risky. Wait until spring, then they'll have all season to settle in.

* Don't assume plants on display at famous gardens have been grown there – more often than not, they have been bought in from a nursery like anywhere else. Plants at small gardens that only open occasionally are more likely to be home-grown.

* Some plants are best bought in flower if they are naturally variable and a particular quality is crucial to your purpose – with hellebores, for example, you can pick out the blackest black, greenest green or best spots.

* If you're buying pot-grown roses in the spring, give them a tug. If they are loose, they have only recently been potted and are best avoided. If firm, they'll have been potted in the autumn – these are the ones to buy.

* Everyone succumbs to impulse buys, but you can make them work for you. Visit specialist nurseries at different times of year, so you don't end up with a garden dominated by plants that flower at the same time. Try visiting garden centres when your garden is at its worst – you should see plenty of plants to inspire you.

* For most trees and shrubs, the smaller and younger the plant the better – they'll cost far less, settle in much quicker, need less aftercare and soon catch up with older plants. Large hedging plants are tempting, but poor value. However, you can make an exception if you want a special slow-growing plant as a focal point, such as a fastigiate yew, Japanese maple or clipped box – £100 spent on one of these can be a real investment.

possible, use a firm that allows you to track the progress of your delivery.

Alternative home-delivery sources for plants and seeds include newspaper and magazine reader offers and online auctions. Although many reader offers focus on the so-called 'Plants of the Year', good deals can be found, especially from the large, well-known firms, such as Thompson and Morgan. Seeds, in particular, are often put up for sale with online auctioneers such as eBay (www.ebay.co.uk). You will run the risk of not really being able to guarantee the quality of the seeds, but you will often secure some amazing bargains. Just make sure you research what you're buying first.

PRIMARY RESOURCES

GARDENING ADVICE WEBSITES

www.bbc.co.uk/gardening
www.expertgardener.com
www.gardenersclub.co.uk/
  mainmenu.html
www.goodgardeners.org.uk
www.hdra.org.uk
www.organicgarden.org.uk
www.rhs.org.uk

GARDENING MAGAZINES

Gardeners' World
  tel: 020 8576 2000
  www.gardenersworld.beeb.com

Gardening Which?
  tel: 0800 252100 quoting GYCC01
  for a free three-month trial
  www.which.net/gardening

Gardens Illustrated
  tel: 01795 414721
  www.gardensillustrated.com

Organic Gardening
  tel: 01984 641212

GARDEN CENTRES

B&Q
  tel: 023 8025 6256
  www.diy.com

Bridgemere Garden World, Cheshire
  tel: 01270 521100
  www.bridgemere.co.uk

Homebase
  tel: 0870 900 8098
  www.homebase.co.uk

Notcutts Garden Centres
  tel: 01394 383344
  www.notcutts.co.uk

Squire's Garden Centres
  tel: 020 8977 9988
  www.squiresgardencentres.co.uk

Van Hage Garden Company
  tel: 01920 870811
  www.vanhage.co.uk

Wyevale
  tel: 0800 413213
  www.wyevale.co.uk

ONLINE RETAILERS

www.blooms-online.com
www.capital-gardens.co.uk
www.crocus.co.uk
www.dig-it.co.uk
www.dobies.co.uk
www.e-garden.co.uk
www.ferndale-lodge.co.uk
www.gardenwise.co.uk
www.greenfingers.com
www.greengardener.co.uk
www.gonegardening.com
www.grogro.com
www.mirrorgarden.co.uk
www.mowdirect.co.uk
www.mowers-online.co.uk
www.mowerworld.co.uk
www.suttons-seeds.co.uk
www.the-plant-directory.com
www.thompson-morgan.com

ASSOCIATIONS

The National Society of
Allotment & Leisure Gardeners
  tel: 01536 266576
  www.nsalg.demon.co.uk

The Permaculture Association
  tel: 07041 390170
  www.permaculture.org.uk

The Royal Horticultural Society
  tel: 020 7834 4333
  www.rhs.org.uk

GARDENING SHOWS

For details of BBC Gardeners' World Live, Chelsea, Hampton Court, Tatton Park and Malvern, visit www.rhs.org.uk/events or ring 020 7834 4333.

property

the basics

This is it: the Big One. We will never make a bigger or more significant purchase in our lives and it's something that, on average, we will end up doing seven times. And with nearly 70 per cent of all adults in the UK able to boast that their name is on the deeds of their home, we justly deserve the tag of a nation of proud homeowners.

But even with interest rates at a record low, ever-spiralling property prices mean that relative affordability is now decreasing faster than the value of a stone-clad bungalow. With mortgage lenders still sticking to their general principle that you can borrow three times your salary – two-and-a-half times your combined salaries if you're a couple – many buyers, particularly first-time buyers, are having to stump up enormous deposits to move onto the property ladder. Therefore, the first task when buying a home is to muster as large a deposit as possible. Easier said than done, admittedly, but it will have a huge bearing on what price range you can end up looking in, as well as what type of mortgage will be available to you.

The other thing to remember in the months before you even start on the road to your dream home is what time of year you begin your search. The speed of the housing market seems to ebb and flow according to the seasons. Spring is traditionally the busiest time for estate agents. It slows in July and August during the school breaks and when people go on holiday. After the kids have gone back to school in September, the market picks up and remains strong until early December when there is an abrupt halt as people turn their mind to Christmas. The rate of sales generally remains sluggish until the following March, when the whole cycle starts again. Therefore, the best time for you to be looking is when the market is slow, and vendors (that's the industry lingo for sellers) might be more willing to take an offer (that's more industry lingo and it means to accept an offer lower than the asking price). Looking at this time of year also means that the estate agents, surveyors, solicitors and all the other people that are key to buying a home should be less busy and have more time for you – in theory.

before you start looking

It's easy, isn't it? You just sign up with a few estate agents and away you go. If only life were that simple. While you want to cast your net as wide as possible so that you don't miss out on your dream home, you also don't want to be wasting time viewing property that is either wholly inappropriate or would require you to mortgage your granny in order to be able to afford it. Estate agents often seem to struggle to grasp this fact.

You should therefore begin by drawing up a realistic and accurate wish-list of what you are looking for so that you can hand it over to the estate agents. This way, hopefully, they can quickly help to find your dream property.

Once you have a settled and realistic idea of what kind of home you want, it's time to organize a mortgage-in-principle. The earlier you have a mortgage agreement in place, the faster the sale will go through and the less chance you'll be leaving yourself open to being gazumped, namely someone coming in and outbidding you after you thought it was a done deal (unless you are lucky enough to live in Scotland where legislation prevents it).

Research your mortgage options as thoroughly as you can. Scour the papers endlessly for the best deals. Get hold of *What Mortgage* magazine (**www.mortgageseekers.co.uk/articles1.htm**) and log on to the MoneyFacts website (**www.moneyfacts.co.uk**) for useful advice and helpful mortgage calculators. Further excellent advice can be found on the Motley Fool's home-owning section at **www.fool.co.uk/homeowning**.

Above all, you're looking for impartial mortgage advice, which sadly is sometimes hard to come by. Stay away from mortgages recommended to you by financial advisors or estate agents, unless you are absolutely sure of their neutrality, as many work on commission. Look out for lenders who have signed up to the Mortgage Code, an industry standard that is meant to guarantee fair advice.

Remember that whoever you end up going with, they will demand that you hand over old bank statements, rental receipts and payslips to help them run credit checks. So make sure all your paperwork is in order, or else it could delay you once you have had an offer accepted.

If you are finding the task of raising enough money for a deposit too much or don't qualify for a 100 per cent mortgage, you could investigate going for a shared-ownership mortgage, whereby you buy a house in partnership with a housing association. For more information about housing associations and how they can help you purchase a home, log on to **www.housingcorp.gov.uk**.

Beyond the headache of working your way through the mortgage maze, you should try and find a good solicitor as early as possible. Estate agents and mortgage lenders will be more than happy to recommend those local to you, but, if you have the time, it is always worth trying to find a wider selection of quotes. If you live in England or Wales, go to **www.solicitors-online.com**, which provides a list of all the solicitors registered with the Law Society. If you're in Scotland, go to **www.lawscot.org.uk**, and in Northern Ireland try **www.lawsoc-ni.org**. All these sites will help you find a local solicitor. Always ask if they are specialists in residential conveyancing, and don't just assume you have to find a solicitor that is based near to your home. Hundreds of pounds can be saved, for example, by using a non-metropolitan solicitor if you want to buy a property in the middle of expensive London.

However, be suspicious of solicitors that offer a really low fixed rate, say £200, for their services, as it could be an indication that they work in bulk and therefore may not offer the thoroughness and speed that you require.

Until the much-vaunted sellers' packs are introduced (which put the onus of the survey on the seller and are promised for 'sometime' in 2003), homebuyers outside Scotland will still have to run the risk of wasting hundreds of pounds on a survey every time a deal falls through. As is the case with solicitors, estate agents and mortgage lenders will help you find a surveyor, but, again, you can save money by finding your own. It sometimes feels as though this cosy triumvirate's relationship is suspiciously close and it can pay to choose one without interference where possible.

If you are searching for a home in an unfamiliar area, it could be worth using the services of a homesearch agent. They don't come cheap (they can charge as much as 1.5 per cent of the sale price), but they can save you a lot of time and effort if briefed well. You can find one through **www.relocationagents.com**.

Finally, before you begin looking in earnest, it's important, if this is relevant, to have established the nature of your relationship with your partner – in writing. Most of us buy a house jointly with someone else, typically our partner, but if the relationship should fail, it is important to have spelt out on paper exactly what will happen to the property. This should be discussed with and drawn up by your solicitor. Your mortgage lender may even demand it.

doing your homework

Now that you are ready to start the search for a home, the emphasis shifts from sorting out your finances and assembling a crack team of buying experts to extensively researching the area in which you want to live.

The important thing to remember is that you cannot do enough research. If the area is alien to you, try to visit it as many times as possible. On weekdays, on weekends, at night and during the day, so you can glean more than just one impression. You also want to log on to as many property sites and read as many local area property guides as possible. You need to establish the following: What's the parking like? What are the schools like? (This is important even if you don't have kids, as it will affect the resale value.) What are the facilities – public transport links, pubs, restaurants, shopping – like? If it is an urban area, is there evidence of gentrification, i.e. coffee bars, gastropubs, property developers?

Traffic-wise, are there rat runs and bottlenecks? What's the local crime rate like? Is the area at risk from flooding or subsidence?

Good places to start are **www.upmystreet.com**, **www.hometrack.co.uk** and the Land Registry's site (**www.landreg.gov.uk/ppr/interactive**). Between these sites, after typing in your target postcode, you will be able to obtain most of the information you need, particularly the pace of the local property market. You could even contact the local planning office to see what is in the pipeline, building-wise, for the area. A good further tip is to type the name of the area into an internet search engine, such as **http://ukyahoo.com**, and just see what it throws up. Many areas now have their own dedicated websites run by residents, which can be extremely useful and even interesting.

If you are considering buying a flat, and hence possibly taking on the joys of dealing with a landlord, it is worth mugging up on exactly what buying a leasehold property entails. The Leasehold Advisory Service's website is a good starting point and can be found at **www.lease-advice.org**, or call 020 7490 9580. Once you have actually had an offer accepted on a flat, it is wise to try and speak to the landlord (if possible, get the number from the vendor or estate agent). A quick phone call can often reveal a lot about what your future relationship may be like.

One last point to consider before setting off on your first viewing is the way some vendors try to make their home look as appealing as possible to you, and in particular, women, as they are seen as the principal decision-makers when couples choose a home. There are lots of completely innocent tricks that have now become almost clichéd – the aroma of freshly brewed coffee, the smell of baking bread – but there are other more devious techniques that have the sole aim of hiding negative aspects of the home. Look out for the following:

* No curtains. Is this because the natural light in the house is not adequate?

* No natural clutter anywhere. Has it all been crammed in a cupboard in an attempt to make rooms look bigger?

* Furniture pushed up against walls. Again, is that really how you

would use a room? Is it another attempt to make a room look bigger?

* Strong-smelling scent. Is the vendor trying to disguise the smell of damp?
* Evidence of recent, localized repainting. Is the vendor trying to disguise a damp patch?

buying from estate agents

The first thing to remember when buying a home via an estate agent is that they're not on your side; their paymaster is the vendor. Their sole interest is convincing you to buy a home as quickly and for as high a price as possible, as this will mean a fatter and faster commission for them. Never forget this.

When it comes to finding an agent, initially you want to register your details with as many as possible in the area in which you're looking. However, try to stick to agents who have signed up to the National Association of Estate Agents' code of conduct (www.naea.co.uk). You may be overwhelmed with property details, but if you have briefed them well about your budget and needs, you should be able to filter out the completely inappropriate properties. Agents have the infuriating habit of pushing properties on people that are thousands beyond the buyer's budget. If an agent continues to do this, they're just wasting your time and you should take your business elsewhere.

Don't just drop in on estate agents unannounced, however. Try to book an appointment in advance, so that they can spend some time listening to your needs. Saturdays are extremely busy days for agents and it's unlikely they will have time for you if you just breeze in looking for instant service.

Watch out, too, for property misdescription. There's a law against it, but the odd fabrication of the truth inevitably creeps into property details. Take all descriptive terms, such as 'in need of modernization' and 'compact and bijou' with the pinch of salt they deserve.

from the web and newspaper classifieds

Looking for property online and in newspapers should always be part of your strategy, as it vastly increases your chances of finding what you want, but think hard before going it alone without the help of an estate agent. In reality, buying privately will mean months of chasing people and worrying that you have done everything you should. If you do want to buy privately, read up about it first at the numerous property advice websites, or in books such as Adam Walker's *Buying a House* or Joseph Bradshaw's *House Buying, Selling and Conveyancing*.

If you are searching for property online, begin by keeping your searches as broad as possible. Typing in your preferred budget and number of bedrooms, for example, means that you can often inadvertently rule out potentially suitable property. Keep the first searches broad, then narrow them down later.

from auctions

Not for the faint-hearted. Auctioneers tend to deal in property that is being sold off by housing associations, councils and banks, usually in a state of disrepair or because of a repossession order. This means that the property will often require considerable structural work, which only property developers will have the means to complete.

Your task is made harder by the fact that you typically have three weeks from the moment the sale catalogue is issued by an auctioneer to the sale itself. In this time you must have had a survey done and have sorted out your mortgage (auctions are not just for cash buyers). As anyone who has bought property will know, to complete that in three weeks will require a Herculean effort.

If you do decide to go ahead, visit some property auctions (find them in the Yellow Pages, or at **www.yell.com**) in advance to gauge how it's done. You will soon notice how most properties tend to go for about 5 to 10 per cent above the guide price in the catalogue. It's therefore important that you have your set budget and that you stick to it.

For further advice on buying at auction, contact Winkworth's auction advice line on 020 8649 7255, or click on 'Auctions' at **www.winkworth.co.uk**.

making an offer

Only you will know what you can afford to offer for a property you want to buy, but it's important that you don't procrastinate. The pace of the market and the location will determine whether the vendor is likely to take an offer, but you can but try.

There are no rules, each case is always different, but offering 5 per cent beneath the asking price is a good ballpark figure to start with. Just make sure that as soon as your offer is expressed (in writing, with 'subject to contract' on it), and then accepted by the vendor, that they take the property off the market immediately. However, agreeing to an 'exclusive' doesn't mean anything until you both sign up to a 'lockout agreement'. In fact, the only other reliable way of preventing yourself from being gazumped is to sign up to a 'pre-contract deposit agreement', which forces one of you to forfeit a prepaid deposit should you pull out of the deal before exchanging contracts.

Once the offer has been accepted, it's time to get your mortgage lender, solicitor and surveyor into action. It's wise to ring them all once a week to chivvy them along, as you don't want anything lingering in an in-tray for days and thus holding the whole process up.

Now is also the time to ring round for your buildings and contents insurance quotes, as the property will need to be covered from the moment you complete. Don't just go with whatever your mortgage lender offers you, as insurance can nearly always be found cheaper after a quick ring-round or browse online. For the same reason, it's worth shopping around for Mortgage Payment Protection Insurance if you think you need it. Many people, however, view this type of insurance with the same scorn as extended warranties, seeing it as an easy way for the lenders to make extra money from you.

Your solicitor will soon send you a list of the property's fixtures and fittings for you to check and sign. Go through this very carefully and don't assume anything is staying: it's common for people to even take light bulbs with them when they move out. You will normally be asked to pay extra for washing machines, cookers and so on, should you want them to remain.

Double-check with your solicitor where any boundaries extend to and about possible public rights of way. Get them to check for any history of disputes between neighbours. If it's a leasehold property, you want to have a precise breakdown and history of service charges. Your solicitor should be doing all this, but it's too important to leave to chance.

Finally, when you have only got a few weeks to go until the magic day of completion when you are handed the keys, log on to **www.ihavemoved.com**. This site saves you a lot of the hassle of telling dozens of people and service providers that you're moving. You should also now contact the Post Office to arrange for your post to be forwarded to your new address. And don't forget to reconfirm your booking with the removal firm about a week before. Your big day would be somewhat scuppered if they failed to show.

PRIMARY RESOURCES

PROPERTY ADVICE AND RESEARCH SITES

www.bbc.co.uk/rightmoves
www.channel4.com/4homes
www.environment-agency.gov.uk
www.iaea.co.uk/infopublic.htm
www.proviser.com
www.reallymoving.com
www.themovechannel.com
http://uk.yell.com/property

PROPERTY-SEARCH SITES

www.activepropertysales.co.uk
www.asserta.co.uk
www.completehousebuyer.co.uk
www.easier.com
www.findaproperty.co.uk
http://fish4.co.uk/homes
www.home.co.uk
www.homefreehome.co.uk
www.homepages.co.uk
www.08004homes.com
www.homes-uk.co.uk
www.hotproperty.co.uk
www.housenet.co.uk

www.houseweb.co.uk
www.itlhomesearch.com
www.primelocation.com
www.propertybroker.co.uk
www.propertyfinder.co.uk
www.propertylive.co.uk
http://property.loot.com
www.property-sight.co.uk
www.property-uk.co.uk
www.propertyworld.com
www.rightmove.co.uk
www.ukpropertyshop.com
www.ukpropertyweb.co.uk
www.wheresforsale.com
www.wheresmyproperty.com

weddings

the basics

The panic. The stress. The tantrums. The expense. We all love a good wedding, but to ensure that divorce papers are not signed the day after the signing of the register, a wedding must be organized with near-military precision. And that includes the budget.

Wedding costs have a habit of expanding faster than a shotgun bride's waistline if left unchecked. When you consider that the average cost of a wedding in the UK now stands at about £11,000 (£14,000 in London), it is easy to see how the smallest miscalculation or oversight can lead to hundreds, if not thousands, of pounds' worth of extra expenditure.

Nobody wants their special day to be cheapened in any way, but there are a number of areas in which prudence should be applied. As soon as the headache of celebrating the engagement wears off, begin by drawing up provisional lists, itineraries and budgets – and start establishing what the priorities are. Handmade new dress or rented? Exotic honeymoon or long weekend in a caravan? Champagne or sparkling wine?

The question that needs answering first, however, is who's footing the bill. Traditionally, the bride's parents pay almost all of the costs, but this is becoming increasingly less common. Alternatively, couples either pay for themselves, or both sets of parents end up sharing the costs. Whatever you decide upon, though, decide early and with absolute clarity. It can be a sensitive question, and a common solution is for the groom's parents to pay for all the food, which, in itself, is a considerable percentage of the wedding's costs.

It is wise to set up immediately a wedding account with your bank in order to closely audit your costs. At a glance, you will be able to see how much you have spent, and whoever is paying can begin to plan how they are going to meet the costs. Remember that you should always budget for at least a 10 per cent overspend.

Also get into the habit of keeping all paperwork, be it invoices, quotes or receipts. Keep details and checklists on a computer and learn to delegate all the responsibilities. It's a good idea, too, to start an ideas folder in which you can keep magazine clippings or styles of dress, flower arrangements and so on that you like, as it will save time when explaining your needs to suppliers.

As most engagements last about twelve months, you should be thinking about numbers of guests and the type of service as soon as possible, as these two factors will obviously have the largest effect on costs. Are you going to have the traditional morning service with a lunch for close family, to be followed by a larger evening do? Or do you prefer the increasingly trendy late afternoon service that imme-diately moves on to the evening reception? Budget-wise, you're best to go with the latter, especially if you do plan on inviting hundreds of guests, as you will then have only one event to manage and pay for.

A weekday wedding will also keep costs down, but is restrictive to many guests. A more realistic solution is possibly to compromise on having a summer wedding. Venues are cheaper to hire in the autumn and winter. A much more contentious, but increasingly considered suggestion is to invite guests to make a financial contribution to your big day, possibly in lieu of presents. Why not disguise this by having a buffet feast and inviting guests to bring a specific dish? Or invite friends and more distant relatives to drinks in the evening instead of a formal meal? Any of these suggestions will significantly reduce the cost of your reception.

You may also opt to use local, small-scale suppliers. The advan-tage of this is that some may not be big enough to register for VAT, because their annual taxable turnover does not exceed £52,000. This will immediately give you a saving of 17.5 per cent. Did you know that wedding cakes (if supplied independently of catering), children's clothing and order of service cards are all exempt from VAT?

But whoever you use and whatever service they provide, get detailed quotes (never estimates) in writing. And if there are supplementary costs, always get the quote updated.

the venue

Whatever type of religious or civil service you want, approach the service venue as early as possible. For example, although only 38 per cent of weddings are now traditional church affairs, many churches can be booked up over a year in advance, especially during the popular late spring and summer months.

Once you have a firm service date, begin your enquiries into which reception venues are available. The reception costs will far outweigh any other cost, and the earlier you put down an advance payment on the reception venue, the better you will be able to confidently organize everything else. After all, it is the linchpin of all your efforts.

Approach each venue with a list of questions to establish whether it is suitable:

* Are you free to use your own suppliers and contractors? Many venues have a preferred list of suppliers, from whom they will, of course, take a commission.

* Are there catering facilities? If not, are there power points for heat trays or portable ovens? It will cost you much more if caterers have to bring all their own equipment.

* What are the transport links and car parking like?

* What are the set-up and clear-up times?

* Is the venue booked by anyone else on that day? Do you really want to risk sharing the venue with, for example, an earlier morning event?

* Are there any decoration or building restrictions? Are you allowed to build a marquee on the lawn? Is smoking permitted? Many older buildings, for example, restrict you from using certain decorations due to the fire risk.

- What time do you have to vacate the building? Is it in a residential area? Are there noise restrictions?
- Will you be charged corkage if you decide to bring your own wine?
- If it is outside, what are the toilet facilities for guests?

catering

The vast majority of weddings are catered for by professionals, and with good reason, but it can be very expensive. Begin by ringing round some local caterers to get an idea of how much it is likely to cost. You must let them know definite numbers, dates and times for them to prepare an accurate quote. Once you have a shortlist, you will also want to visit them, read through references, and, ideally, look at photographs of past events for which they have catered. When you are talking money, establish what deposit they require, when they want the final bill to be settled and whether they will also charge for corkage should you supply your own wine.

Again, you will need to arm yourself with an additional checklist of questions:

- Will the caterers do all of the clearing-up?
- Will they provide all the catering equipment they need, as well as all the cutlery, glasses, table linen and crockery?
- Are they providing the cake stand and knife?
- How much notice do they need for the final number of guests?
- Will they cater for every dietary need?

If you wish to reduce costs without appearing too cheap, think about a buffet. You can have the same standard of food for half the price. (Sit-down meals usually start at about £20 a head, buffets start at £10 a head.) Or what about a 'novelty' meal? Over the last couple of years, it has been become popular to serve guests bangers and mash (like Kate Winslet), or fish and chips.

You could also save on costs by ringing a local catering college to see whether they, instead of the professional caterers, could provide the waiting staff. They may even offer a good price to provide the food itself.

wedding costs: a breakdown

Here's where weddingguideuk.com says the money is spent on an average wedding:

	£
Bride's wedding ring	200
Groom's wedding ring	150
Wedding dress	700
Headdress and veil	150
Bridal bouquet	75
Shoes and accessories	125
Bride's beauty treatments	75
Bridesmaids' dresses	500
Groom's outfit	150
Flowers (buttonholes, church etc)	200
Printing	300
Transportation	300
Civil/church fees	200
Photography	400
Videography	400
Wedding cake	200
Reception venue or marquee hire	600
Reception decorations	150
Wedding reception catering	2,000
Evening reception catering	750
Drinks	750
Entertainment	500
Bride's going-away outfit	150
Wedding-night hotel	125
Honeymoon	1,500
Wedding insurance	50
Other expenses	300
Total	**£11,000**

Many people now organize their own alcohol with a 'booze cruise' beforehand. It's a sensible option, but one that should be carefully costed. How much will the fuel, ferry crossing and any vehicle hire amount to? It's up to you whether you insist on champagne, but a good-quality Australian sparkling wine, for example, will cost significantly less, and the vast majority of guests will not notice the difference.

invitations

To get a printer or stationery firm to print one hundred invitations on quality card, you should expect to pay about £200. You can therefore see how quickly printing costs can add up, especially once you add the printing of the order of service, menus and place names for the tables.

Invitations need to be ordered at least three months ahead of the wedding and sent out about a month later. You should probably print about 5 per cent extra to allow for any last-minute guests, but make sure you examine the proofs carefully, as any mistakes spotted beyond this point will be at your expense. The Craft Council (see 'primary resources') will give you a list of stationers in your area. You could, of course, write out your own invites – or print them via a home PC – to save on costs.

the dress

As one of the most personal choices of a wedding, this one is up to you. Do you go for traditional, modern, hired, handmade, off-the-peg, white, ivory...? Whichever you choose, the earlier you decide, the better the deal you will secure. To help make a choice, visit a wedding show and your local bridal shops. Ask shops when their next sale is likely to be.

It's virtually impossible to give an average price for a wedding dress, but a second-hand dress could cost as little as £100, while ready-to-wear dresses from Debenhams, for example, cost between £100 and £450, and custom-made designer dresses cost upwards of £1,000. Hiring dresses will cost between £80 and £500, with the average cost being about £200.

When you have found a handful of shops, try to make a fitting appointment as soon as possible (you'll need at least an hour), and preferably not on a Saturday, when they will be at their busiest.

Most grooms hire a suit, typically a morning suit, but it may be worth investing a bit more money in a new suit that could be used again in the future, because renting a wedding suit costs about £100 a day.

And don't forget that outfits for any bridesmaids or pageboys are likely to cost you up to £100 per outfit.

the flowers

The cost of flowers takes many couples by surprise. To pay for flowers at the service, the reception and for the bride costs upwards of £200. The bride's bouquet alone can cost up to £100 (and to think it ends up just being tossed over the bride's shoulder...). To help save on florist's costs, see if any members of your family are willing to do the arranging. Many churches will have their own flower arrangers who may do it cheaper than a florist. You may even be able to make a contribution to their regular weekly flower costs if they can leave the flowers behind for your service. And remember that if other services are taking place at the same venue on the same day, you could all share the flower costs.

Flowers at the reception, particularly around the cake, are still popular. When visiting local florists, avoid busy Saturdays and ask to see examples of their previous work. Flowers that are currently popular for weddings are freesias, gerberas, ivy, jasmine, arum lilies and, of course, roses. Contact the British Retail and Professional Florists Association (see 'primary resources') for advice on wedding flowers and the location of affiliated florists. It's a long shot, but some nurseries hire out their plants for special occasions, so ring round.

the photographer

Not an area where most would want to cut corners, but as ever, ask to see references and examples of their work. The Guild of Wedding Photographers (see 'primary resources') will help you find local

get me to the church on time: wedding coordinators

For some, the challenge of organizing a wedding is too much. Getting in a professional to help will save you time, but more importantly could actually save you money. A wedding coordinator will typically charge upwards of £500 for organizing the entire wedding, but they will be able to negotiate a range of discounts from preferred suppliers that would otherwise be out of your reach.

You will need to negotiate with them exactly what their fee includes. Some charge by the hour, some will quote a total for the job, and some charge a set percentage of the final cost of the wedding.

You can, of course, get a coordinator in to help with a single task, such as booking a reception venue, but always consider what the likely saving will be from your investment.

Whoever you use, let them know as soon as possible about your tastes and ideas (haven't you seen Jennifer Lopez in *The Wedding Planner*?), and try to speak to couples who have used the coordinator before. All coordinators should let you look through references and thank-you notes.

affiliated photographers. The Guild says that prices depend on the total time the photographer spends at your wedding, the approximate number of photographs to be taken, the number of pictures included in any package deal (not necessarily the same thing), and the type and quality of the album. The Guild warns that you should be wary of any package that contains, say, twenty photographs from a selection of twenty-four. The photographer is not offering much leeway for mistakes.

A cheap and novel way of getting a wider range of photographs is to leave disposable cameras on every table and ask guests to use the film in any way they want. You can then collect the cameras at the end of the reception.

the cake

With most traditional wedding cakes costing up to £200, there are a few tricks to keeping costs down. Instead of asking for quotes on wedding cakes when you are making your enquiries, simply ask for prices on 'occasion' cakes. These are usually very similar – fruit cake with intricate icing – but are cheaper. You can ask a friend or relative to personalize it. It is even cheaper to ask a relative or friend to make the cake, and then get the professionals in to ice it. The British Sugar Craft Guild (see 'primary resources') should be able to give you advice.

transport

Horse and carriage? Limousine? Helicopter? Minicab? However you choose to get to your wedding, make sure you actually see the transport in question, rather than just photos, before paying any deposit. Photos will not show dents and scratches. Confirm your booking at least a week before the event to make sure it hasn't been double-booked and don't forget transport for the rest of the bridal party.

Remember, too, to ask around to see whether there's a friend of a friend who will lend you their posh car for the day.

honeymoon

This is traditionally the groom's responsibility, but whoever is booking the honeymoon should always mention to the travel agents and airlines that honeymooners are travelling. It is probably the one time in your life when you could realistically expect perks, the odd upgrade and special treatment.

wedding insurance

Don't get married without it. It should only cost you, on average, between £50 and £100, but will cover the cost of double bookings, damage to the dress, theft of presents, cancellations due to illness and the like. What it will not cover, however, is the consequences of cold feet.

---

expert view

Sandy Boler, editor of *Brides* magazine, says you should remember the following points when planning for your big day:

* The first decisions are crucial: when, where and how you want to marry. Religious or civil ceremony? Large or small? Town or country? What time of year?

* Be realistic about how much the wedding might cost, and whether you want or can expect financial help from your parents. Decide as much as you can together, so that your minds are clear before you involve others, but be prepared to listen to their ideas, especially if they are the hosts.

* Keep a sense of proportion – if your original choice of venue is not possible, there will be other excellent possibilities. The new, slightly relaxed, church laws and the enormous variety of licensed venues provide a wide range to choose from.

* Never try to persuade anyone who does not want to be best man to change their mind. Choose a friend or relative who would feel confident in the role. Never be persuaded to have a bridesmaid you don't really want.

* Tread carefully with the guest list – the new trend of inviting a larger proportion of friends of the couple makes sense. They are the people whose support you will need in the future.

* Remember the golden rule: most speeches would be twice as good if they were half as long.

PRIMARY RESOURCES

ONLINE WEDDING ADVICE AND SHOPPING DIRECTORIES

www.confetti.co.uk
www.getspliced.com
www.hitched.co.uk
www.scottishweddings.org
www.weddingguideuk.com
www.wedding-service.co.uk
www.weddingservices4u.co.uk
www.wedseek.co.uk

BRIDAL MAGAZINES

Bride and Groom
tel: 020 7437 0796
www.brideandgroommag.co.uk

Brides
tel: 020 7499 9080
www.bridesuk.net

You and Your Wedding
tel: 020 7439 5000
www.youandyourwedding.co.uk

USEFUL TRADE ASSOCIATIONS

British Retail and Professional Florists Association
tel: 01992 767645

British Sugar Craft Guild
tel: 020 8859 6943
www.bsguk.org

The Crafts Council
tel: 020 8859 6943
www.craftscouncil.org.uk

The Flowers & Plants Association
tel: 020 7738 8044
www.flowers.org.uk

Guild of Wedding Photographers
tel: 0161 926 9367
www.gwp-uk.co.uk

BRIDAL SHOWS

The London Wedding Show
www.wedding-expo.com

Silverlinings
tel: 01832 731173
www.silverlinings.co.uk

The UK Wedding Show @ Wembley (held annually in September)
tel: 01704 833207
www.confettiandco.co.uk

Wedding Fayres
tel: 01625 610004
www.weddingfayres.co.uk

WEDDING COORDINATORS

Milestone Weddings
tel: 020 8488 7223
www.milestoneweddings.co.uk

Virgin Bride
tel: 020 7321 0866
www.virgin.com/bride

The Wedding Design Studio
tel: 01795 439970
www.weddingdesignstudio.co.uk

The Wedding Event Company
tel: 01536 744141
www.theweddingeventcompany.co.uk

ADDITIONAL READING

There are hundreds of books aimed at guiding you through a wedding. Just type in 'weddings' at www.amazon.co.uk. The *Which? Guide to Getting Married* is published by *Which?* Books and costs £9.99. Call 0800 252100.

wine

the basics

For the vast majority of us, buying wine means staring at a super-market shelf trying to match a nice-looking label with a nice-looking price. In the UK, this increasingly means a New World Cabernet or Chardonnay priced at between £4 and £5. Isn't this rather sad for a nation that has such a long and proud wine-buying history?

Of course, the mystique and mythology of wine doesn't help. All that 'I taste manure and loganberries' by wine critics seems to have only inhibited an already nervy wine-buying public and led many of us to stick to what we know best, or rather what the supermarkets know best. This is a shame, as with care, buying wine away from the high street can be rewarding, as well as – potentially – a good investment.

It is important, however, to make your mind up early on: do you want to buy wine to drink, or to make money? It is possible to combine the two, but buying wine as an investment is a serious business that is most profitable when the wine is sold on without you ever having handled it.

buying wine to drink

The well-stocked wine cellar is a fantasy for most of us. Only a handful of homes really have adequate storage room or the correct conditions to keep large quantities of wine at home for drinking or laying down. Most of us have to put up with a small wine rack in the kitchen or under the stairs, which isn't exactly conducive to building up a decent collection. This means that a few cases is all that we can realistically have in the house at any one time, and this limits where and how you can buy wine.

Beyond the high street (which can still offer exceptional deals on cases if you hunt around and wait for special offers), many novice wine buyers are drawn to wine clubs. The *Sunday Times* Wine Club is, perhaps, the best-known, but they all work on the same principle: you pay a small annual subscription to be regularly informed about well-priced wines that have been vetted and recommended by the club's experts. The combined buying power of a club that boasts a few thousand members allows it to secure some great deals. The bigger clubs offer a vast range of wines, and most sell the ever-popular mixed cases, so all in all, buying through a wine club is a safe and sensible way to buy wine for the average, low-volume private buyer.

The other popular method to secure some real bargain prices is to head across the Channel to Calais's pile 'em high superstores. When you consider that every bottle of wine in the UK, regardless of its retail price, earns £1.16 for the chancellor's coffers (the French pay 2p a bottle, the Germans nothing), it is clear where much of the saving comes from.

Two million of us go on booze cruises every year in search of cheap deals. Most go with a car or van to stock up before special occasions (parties, weddings, Christmas), but if you don't want to pay for your vehicle to travel across the Channel, consider Hoverspeed's 'select and collect' scheme, which allows you to select from a catalogue before you leave the UK. As long as you travel over as a passenger, Hoverspeed do the rest, such as picking up the wine then shipping it back to Dover for you.

Do your research before you head over, though. The last thing you want to be doing is fighting with the crowds while trying to comparison-shop. Check out **www.day-tripper.net** for prices and further advice before you go, such as not going on Sundays when most shops will be shut.

In fact, over the last few years, more and more wine buyers have turned to the net: not just to do their homework, but also to buy. There are hundreds of online retailers out there, but as with buying most products online, stick to the well-known, long-established names (see 'primary resources').

Many of them operate in a similar way to the wine clubs, in that they offer mixed cases, bin ends (end-of-line offers) and regular cases of well-received plonk. You may need to hunt around a bit harder for retailers that sell older, rarer wines, but only do so if you really know what you're buying, or are well advised. It's best, really, to stick with websites that are just the online presence of a trusted bricks-and-mortar retailer. And don't forget that non-UK-based retailers may look cheap, but you will need to pay tax and duty on your purchase.

buying wine as an investment

This is where things start to get serious. It's one thing hunting down the odd bargain case of wine for drinking at home. It's another when you're trying to make serious profit from wine.

The good news is that if you're in it for the long haul, investing in wine can (please note the emphasis on 'can') reap a healthy return on your initial investment: in some cases, much better than more traditional stock market investments. The bad news is that it is a fickle, high-risk market that is determined by the opinion of all-powerful critics.

You should really be looking to wait at least five years before realizing any profit, but ideally, a 10- to 20-year investment period is best. If you're after a quick profit, forget it, but wine can be a good nest egg for retirement, mortgage pay-offs and school fees. What's more, it's largely a tax-free investment if you play it right.

Most brokers recommend a minimum investment of £3,000. Whatever you can afford, stick to the highest-quality wines. Ideally, this will mean classic claret from the 'first-growth' vineyards of Bordeaux: Châteaux Cheval-Blanc (Saint-Emilion), Haut-Brion (Pessac-Léognan), Lafite-Rothschild (Pauillac), Latour (Pauillac), Margaux (Margaux), Mouton-Rothschild (Pauillac) and Pétrus (Pomerol).

If these wines are out of reach (the latest vintages will cost over £1,000 a case), then consider other red Bordeaux classed growths, the best vintage ports from 'British' houses and the very best Burgundy. Down from this, but getting increasingly risky for investment purposes, are the best red Rhônes, the very best Italian wines (from Piedmont and Tuscany) and exceptional wines from California and Australia.

Don't buy anything without knowing exactly what you are doing. Better still, work with a specialist at a trusted broker (see 'primary resources'). Alternatively, you could look at **www.uvine.com**, the first stock exchange for wine, run by a former head of wine at Christie's, but you won't get the expert advice required to build up a good portfolio.

Popular long-term portfolios include building up 'horizontal' or 'vertical' collections. A horizontal collection is when you collect every size of bottle offered by a vineyard in a particular year. This means collecting a complete set of, say, Château Margaux 2000, namely half-bottles, normal bottles, magnums, jeroboams and Nebuchadnezzars. The larger bottles take longer to mature and will usually yield better profits over time.

A vertical collection is when you collect a running sequence of vintages from a particular vineyard. There is a school of thought that some vintages have a certain allure, such as the year 2000. Just as the 1900 vintage tends to command better prices than 1899 and 1901, some feel that, in time, the 2000 vintage will be a stronger seller simply because it represents the turn of the millennium. In terms of quality, however, weather conditions determine the best vintages. These are universally acknowledged, and information about them is easy to obtain online or through a broker.

Whichever broker you use, you will soon hear about buying wine *en primeur*. This is when you buy wine before it has even been bottled. Every March, the leading critics head to Bordeaux to taste and grade last summer's casked wine. This is when a year's vintage is judged and when its reputation is first formed. Commentators such as Robert Parker, the US critic who probably holds more sway over the wine market than anyone else, appraise the different offerings from the vineyards, and as soon as they make their views known, the *en primeur* prices are released.

Buying *en primeur* has seen some extraordinary returns since the 1970s, but in the last three or four years, some first-growth clarets have actually seen a loss, so beware. Do your homework and make sure you shop around the leading brokers for the best rates of commission.

Good places to start when researching broker tips are **www.wine-searcher.com**, which lets you determine the common retail price of most wines and vintages, and **www.investdrinks.org**, which names and shames all the bogus wine brokers (there have been many in recent years), as well as offering solid advice on wine investments.

Robert Parker's influence on the wine market shouldn't be ignored. You can be first to know of his *en primeur* gradings (out of 100) by subscribing to his newsletter (about £50 a year from **www.wineadvocate.com**). It might also pay to subscribe to a wine magazine such as *Decanter* to keep up with the market movements, and if you feel you could do with a beginner's course, contact the Wine and Spirit Education Trust.

Whether you consider it a good thing that critics should exercise such a powerful influence over the wine market is almost irrelevant. You're in it to make money, not taste good wine. In fact, if you plan on taking your profits tax-free (who doesn't?), then you won't even see the wine you buy, as it will remain stored 'under bond' at a warehouse.

For about £7 a year per case, your wine will be correctly stored and insured by one of these wine warehouses (the best-known in the UK is probably Octavian). While there, it will be exempt from VAT and customs and excise duty. If you sell it on while the wine remains under bond, you won't have to pay any tax. It's only when someone decides to take it out of storage that the taxman cometh.

buying at auction

Everyone who has invested in wine needs to sell it at some point to reap their profits. Many will simply sell it straight back to a broker,

ethics watch: corks

When *Ethical Consumer* magazine researched wine corks, it was concerned about the trend towards using plastic. The withdrawal from natural cork use threatens not only the livelihoods of the estimated twenty-five thousand people employed in the cork industry, but also the cork trees themselves and a high number of endangered bird species that live amid cork trees.

European cork comes from the bark of the tree *Quercus suber*, and is grown primarily in Spain and Portugal. The areas where the trees are grown, known as *dehesas*, are inextricably connected to many other species, and campaigns by the RSPB and Birdlife International have been set up to ensure the crop is preserved.

Suppliers who could guarantee that all the wines they sold used cork and not plastic were: Roger's Fine Wine, Vincemeros, Vintage Roots Ltd and The Organic Wine Company.

For more information, visit www.ethicalconsumer.org or call 0161 226 2929.

who will, in turn, sell it on again for additional profit. Another way people choose to offload their portfolios is through an auction.

Wine that is still under bond can be auctioned without ever leaving the warehouse and hence the seller takes their profit tax-free. Alternatively, many people choose to auction off their own cellars, as Andrew Lloyd Webber famously did in the mid-1990s.

Auction houses that hold wine sales (see 'primary resources') tend to stick to dealing with rare, expensive wines. If you are looking for a potential bargain, doing your homework is more important than ever. You will be up against professional dealers in most cases, and will need to really know the true potential and quality of the lots being offered.

If you're a novice, go along to an auction first just to see how it operates. Buy a catalogue and, once back at home, research the wines being offered. When you return, you will need to register before you'll be allowed to bid. Don't forget that a 'buyer's premium' – the auction house's percentage – will be added to the price accepted, and that if you want an under-bond wine to take home to drink, you will have to pay the tax beforehand.

Remember, too, that when wines from the same vineyard are offered, the best quality will be auctioned first. Whoever successfully bids for the first lot of that wine will have the option of buying the rest at the same price. It may not always pay off to hold on until the end.

expert view

Jamie Goode, editor of **wineanorak.co.uk**, passes on his tips for the savvy wine buyer:

* How much do you want to spend? At £5 and under, the market is dominated by branded wines. The likes of Lindemans, Hardy's and Jacob's Creek make accessible, fruity, crowd-pleasing wines – safe territory, if a little uniform and dull. If you really must buy branded wines, two tips: Aussie brands are generally better than their Californian counterparts, and brands rely on regular promotions, so wait for these and then stock up.

* Cheap wine doesn't need to be boring. For more interesting wines that won't break the bank, the south of France leads the field. Other good bets are southern Italy (Puglia, Sicily), Portugal and Spain.

* Pushing the boat out? You'll need to work a little harder. Wine's increasing popularity means that the good stuff is getting difficult to find. Interesting wines from small producers – real geek fodder – aren't made in the quantities required by supermarkets and high-street outlets, so you'll need to use the smaller specialist wine merchants. Most do mail order.

* If you live in striking distance of a decent independent wine merchant, take advantage of your good fortune by building a relationship with them. They'll get to know your palate and be able to advise you better, and you'll be the first to know of any special wines that don't make the shelves.

* If you're relatively new to wine, don't stock up too heavily on your favourite tipple, because your palate will change over time. You don't want to be left with a cellar full of Aussie Shiraz if your true passion ends up being domaine-bottled Burgundy.

* Plundering the sales: each January and August, many merchants have bin-end sales, when they get rid of excess stock. But you usually have to move quickly.

* Critics are useful, but don't follow them slavishly. Your palate may differ from theirs, and wine isn't as exact a science as some would have you believe.

* Do your homework before you buy. The key to wine quality is the name of the producer, not the name of the region or the grape.

PRIMARY RESOURCES

GENERAL WINE ADVICE SITES

www.cyberbacchus.com
www.jancisrobinson.com
www.superplonk.com
www.wineadvocate.com
www.wineanorak.com
www.wineloverspage.com
www.wine-pages.com
www.winepros.co.uk

WINE MAGAZINES

Decanter
www.decanter.com

Wine Spectator
www.winespectator.com

WINE INVESTMENT BROKERS

Magnum Fine Wines
tel: 020 7839 5732
www.magnum.co.uk

Premier Cru Investments
tel: 020 8905 4495
www.premiercru.com

Quest Wine Investments
tel: 01256 760862
www.investment-wines.com

WINE 'STOCK EXCHANGE'

Uvine
tel: 0800 328 8448
www.uvine.com

WINE-PRICE SEARCH ENGINES

www.wine-searcher.com

BONDED WAREHOUSES

Octavian
tel: 01225 810735
www.octavian.co.uk/octavian.htm

WINE ASSOCIATIONS

Institute of Masters of Wine
tel: 020 7236 4427
www.masters-of-wine.org

Wine and Spirit Association
tel: 020 7248 5377
www.wsa.org.uk

Wine and Spirit Education Trust
tel: 020 7236 3551
www.wset.co.uk

AUCTION HOUSES

Christie's
tel: 020 7839 9060
www.christies.com

Sotheby's
tel: 020 7293 5000
www.sothebys.co.uk

WINE CLUBS

Sunday Times Wine Club
tel: 0870 220 0010
www.sundaytimeswineclub.co.uk

The Wine Society
tel: 01438 761201

The Wine Treasury
tel: 020 7793 9999
www.winetreasury.com

ONLINE RETAILERS

www.armit.co.uk
www.bbr.com
www.bibendum-wine.co.uk
www.chateauonline.co.uk
www.everywine.co.uk
www.itswine.com
www.laithwaites.co.uk
www.madaboutwine.com
www.majestic.co.uk
www.oddbins.com
www.safeway.co.uk
www.sainsburys.co.uk
www.tesco.co.uk
www.virginwines.com
www.winecellar.co.uk